Painters, Philosophers and Poets
Sustain a Seven-year Cycle

Lyn Drummond

Painters, Philosophers and Poets Sustain a Seven-year Cycle

Thanks to Sarah Pickette, Judith Mandy, Linda Elliott,
Shaun Drummond, Geoff Mitchell, Duncan Peattie
and Antonia Burrows for their advice and encouragement

To my family and friends

Painters, Philosophers and Poets Sustain a Seven-year Cycle
ISBN 978 1 76109 309 8
Copyright © text Lyn Drummond 2022
Cover image: the author on the historic Avignon bridge in France, made famous in the song 'Sur le Pont d'Avignon'

First published 2022 by
GINNINDERRA PRESS
PO Box 3461 Port Adelaide 5015
www.ginninderrapress.com.au

Contents

Contents	5
Introduction	9
1 When mother knows best	11
2 Vietnam and Know One Teach One	14
3 Santiago, Ecuador and the Galapagos	19
4 Detours, reunions and closures	24
5 The Hague, August 2012–March 2014	28
6 The Peace Palace	29
7 Macedonia and its new name	31
8 Art and philosophy on my doorstep	33
9 Tulipmania	35
10 Baruch Spinoza	37
11 Religion, nature and spirituality	40
12 My French farce, March 2014	44
13 Cézanne and Mont Sainte-Victoire	50
14 Van Gogh in Arles	53
15 Amsterdam, June 2014–October 2015	56
16 Shipbuilder Peter the Great	58
17 Drugs and prostitution	60
18 Friesland and Mata Hari	62
19 Thinking of moving on?	64
20 New Orleans, April 2015	66
21 Cajun and Creole	68
22 Horn-tootin' steamboat captains	70
23 Melbourne, October 2015–June 2017	72
24 Interest on maturity	74
25 Asylum seekers squat in empty buildings	79

26	Former refugee boats cruise Amsterdam canals	85
27	On the sustainable honey highway	88
28	Volunteering exploits experience	91
29	Hungary and medical tourism, 2017	93
30	Poet Edward Thomas and Adlestrop	95
31	Budapest, September 2017	99
32	The benefits of HRT	101
33	The cycle ends, 2018	103
34	Budapest, March 2022	106
	Bibliography	109

'The investigation of nature in general is the basis of philosophy'
– Baruch Spinoza

'Painting from nature is not copying the object, it's realising one's sensations' – Paul Cézanne

'…and then, I have nature and art and poetry, and if that is not enough, what is enough?' – Vincent Willem van Gogh

Introduction

Unlike my previous book, *Where To Go For a Seven-year Cycle*, which mainly focused on my travels from 2003 to 2010 in a specific region – central and eastern Europe – *Painters, Philosophers and Poets Sustain a Seven-year Cycl*e highlights more random locations from 2011 to 2018. It tells stories of how I shared my footprint with the ghosts of famous people such as painters, philosophers and poets who coincidentally lived in the same places as myself, often eras apart from one another. The books' titles are based on philosophical views that seven years of our lives represent a particular cycle.

What I learned from some of the people in this book affected my own perspectives. For example, researching the work of seventeenth-century philosopher Baruch Spinoza, who lived near my home in The Hague, resulted in scrutiny of my beliefs about religion, nature and spirituality. Searching for reasons why Paul Cézanne was so enamoured with Mont Sainte-Victoire, which overlooks the artist's home city of Aix-en-Provence, triggered strong reactions to compelling landscapes. The book examines the influence American poet Robert Frost had on Edward Thomas, the British poet, essayist and novelist who wrote a poem that struck an evocative chord with a nation on the brink of World War I.

My journeys took me from the bleak reality of war crime trials at The Hague International Criminal Tribunal for the former Yugoslavia to the cobbled charm of Arles, the French city where the Dutch painter Van Gogh flourished. To places as diverse as Vietnam and Ecuador, North Macedonia and Louisiana, the Netherlands and Hungary. Uncovering facts hitherto unknown to me about renowned figures such as Tsar Peter the Great of Russia, Albert Einstein, Ho Chi Minh, Alexander the Great, Mata Hari, the last Creole plantation owner, Laura Locoul Gore, and the Hungarian pioneer of Covid-19 vaccines, Dr Katalin Karikó.

Why seven cycles? Searching for a title for the earlier book after completing seven years of travelling, I discovered that in bygone days the number seven was regarded as a mystical or sacred number. Composed of four and three, these numbers were lucky to the ancient Pythagoreans. There are seven days in the week, seven graces, seven deadly sins, and the seventh son of a seventh son was considered noble. William Shakespeare's famous soliloquy from *As You Like It* that begins 'All the world's a stage' presents seven stages or cycles in life.

The Swiss psychiatrist Carl Jung developed a theory about cycles of life he called individuation. He believed that realising individuation was a journey towards completely understanding ourselves. More specifically, answering the question of who we really are beneath our responsibilities and social roles. Once we took off the masks that we hid behind. Once we had faced up to all our hidden secrets and made peace with our darkest corners. Daring to be ourselves no matter how different we were from others.

Although the first story about my mother inspiring my thirst for adventure when I was fifteen does not fit with the cycle's timeline, it is important because it propelled me into a continuing search for the inner assurance that Jung described.

1

When mother knows best

My mother often had uncanny foresight. The most significant for my future happened when I was fifteen. I disliked school immensely and intended to leave at sixteen, despite having no idea of what I might do. It was a notice in our local weekly newspaper, in England, *The Harwich and Manningtree Standard*, which motivated my lifelong vocation. A reporter on the newspaper had become engaged to a British soldier. My mother thought it would be a great idea if I wrote to the editor expressing my interest in a job the following year when I turned sixteen. That reporter might well get married within a year and then go with her new husband to a posting overseas, she reasoned. I was sceptical but after some thought – English was my best subject – I wrote to the editor. As I expected, there were no vacancies, but he would keep my letter on file.

The editor called me in for an interview near the end of my last few months at school. There was a vacancy. As my mother had predicted, the reporter had married and she and her soldier husband were being posted to Germany. If my three-month trial period was a success, I would be offered a four-year indentured journalism apprenticeship.

I started my new job the day after leaving school. But the vacancy had been very aptly filled by a twenty-four-year-old for seven years – shoes almost impossible to fill in three months. In my regular rounds, I saw police, undertakers, a cobbler, the local priests, fire brigade, all the usual suspects for hopefully a good story. It wasn't working. Unimpressed, the editor urged me to try harder. I told my mother.

Angry, she went to see him, despite my mortified protests. She gave me no details but I can imagine what was said. My often unassuming mother could be very feisty. 'How can you expect a sixteen-year-old to fill the shoes of an experienced journalist by being thrown in the deep end without sufficient training?' or words to that effect.

I arrived at work the next day expecting to be fired. Instead, I was given a new assignment. To write a theatre review. The editor said my review was spot on with its unusual angle. My future was secured. Despite my objections, he had once refused to send me to fatal road crashes and other confronting events because I was 'too young'. His attitude eventually changed. I continued my general rounds for story ideas but with a different attitude from one of slight apathy as to the point of them. How do you get a story from an undertaker? In the past, I had often been tempted to skip dropping by but Ernie was a treat to chat to and you never knew,

Then it happened. The undertaker's nephew Mick Oldroyd had joined the popular 1960s pop group Manfred Mann and changed his name to Mick Rogers. What a great local-boy-makes-good story. (I later met Mick again at a Manfred Mann concert in Brisbane after emigrating to Australia in 1966.) Then there was the glamour of interviewing pop stars like Adam Faith and Billy J. Kramer on their way through my patch to the pirate radio ships anchored in the North Sea.

At seventeen, an accidental encounter with Elizabeth Taylor and Richard Burton at the port of Harwich gave me the chance to be the only journalist who was able to interview them. Burton had been in Germany filming *The Spy Who Came In From the Cold*. My chief of staff had asked me to go with him just for a look while he attempted an interview – then neatly stepped behind me. I was the only print journalist among the TV cameras facing the famous pair when they emerged from Customs. I babbled obvious questions about the film. Then Burton, who seemed keen to put me at ease, talked about the experience and future plans while Taylor tugged at his arm, urging him to get on the train to London. She was stunning, petite in a pink suit and matching boater. I was on a high. On TV that night. In my newspaper.

But my euphoria did not please everyone. The Catholic priest I vis-

First scoop as a seventeen-year-old trainee journalist in England. An interview with Elizabeth Taylor and Richard Burton on their return from Germany, where Burton had been making the film The Spy Who Came In From the Cold.

ited on my rounds for story leads and to share his daily tipple of whiskey – very small for me – refused to let me into the presbytery after reading the article. He said he had no intention of talking to someone who had lowered their moral standards to chat with 'such a hussy as Elizabeth Taylor'. Needless to say, my mother was thrilled. But it was only after she died in 2010 that I discovered she had kept those long-ago press photographs and many more charting my career in England, Australia and many other countries.

2

Vietnam and Know One Teach One

I had never considered going to Vietnam. My experiences of south-east Asian countries were usually two- or three-day stopovers to or from Europe and I had no strong desire to explore further. But I did not hesitate when offered the chance to work in Hanoi during a summer recess in 2010 while studying for my master's degree in international relations at Sydney's Macquarie University. The university coordinated the program with Australian Volunteers International at Know One Teach One (KOTO), a hospitality training school for disadvantaged young people.

In 1998, Vietnamese-Australian Jimmy Pham set up a not-for-profit organisation called Street Voices. Working with street children, he opened a sandwich shop in Hanoi a year later. In 2007, Street Voices was renamed KOTO, underlining its philosophy that knowledge is meant to be shared. Since then, KOTO has given innumerable at-risk youth a chance of a career with the help of donations, sponsors, volunteers and staff. Students who receive their qualifications from Australia's Box Hill Institute in Melbourne have often won scholarships to other countries. Jimmy Pham, who I met for the first time in 2011, a few months after working for KOTO, believes that his venture was an opportunity for young people to improve not only their lives, but those of their families and often their communities.

Children and youth end up on the street for different reasons. Some have escaped from broken families or domestic violence. As Jimmy Pham explained, they do not have full knowledge of their rights and often are unaware of the risks in city life. Although visible on the streets, they are also among the most 'invisible' and hence the hardest young people to reach with services such as education or healthcare, and the most difficult to protect. Their future is limited, as suggested by the Vietnamese name for them: Bui-Do – 'dust of life'.

I flew Vietnam Airlines to Ho Chi Minh City in the country's southern region for a brief stopover en route to Hanoi. We left at midday in Sydney, nine a.m. in Ho Chi Minh City, so I was ready for plenty of sky and, hopefully, land watching from my window seat. Instead, it was darkness almost the whole way. As soon as the aircraft lifted above the clouds, flight attendants told us to pull down window blinds, dimmed lights and bade us a good sleep. No explanation. Made worse by the easy acceptance of the snoring passengers near me. It was a relief to pull up the blinds as we neared our destination and I could see spread out below one teeming part of Vietnam's largest and most populous city; the metropolitan area alone has some eight million people. Ho Chi Minh City, which is still commonly known as Saigon, shares a frustrating similarity with Hanoi – its torrent of motor scooter traffic and rare crossing lights – although drivers usually ignored red lights. 'Just

Walking past Vietnam's biggest theatre – Hanoi's stately neoclassical opera house.

walk out onto the road,' I was advised. 'They will drive around you.' They did – just. Often with children hanging on in front or riding pillion with no protection.

Ho Chi Minh was the founding father of modern Vietnam who, despite leading the country's communist revolution against French colonial rule and then taking on the United States, asserted it was patriotism, not communism, that inspired him. Ho and his top general, Vo Nguyen Giap, modelled their war to some extent on George Washington's fight against the British: wear down the enemy, avoid catastrophic defeat, and make it too expensive for your superior enemy to continue the battle. Ho once lived in Boston and New York City, often using pseudonyms in his work as a cook or baker. One prominent place was Boston's Parker House Hotel, whose guests had included Charles Dickens.

While many of the best attractions in Ho Chi Minh City centred on the events of twentieth-century war and conquest, the French colonial history was particularly predominant in the capital, Hanoi. I liked it immediately. The capital, located in the country's north, has a welcoming atmosphere which combines its cultural French and Chinese influences with Vietnamese hospitality and local traditions. My group stayed in a hotel, often in rooms with no windows.

Every morning in the steamy heat of July and August, we walked to the KOTO school. I taught life skills and worked with the social welfare team on specific programs. We regularly visited the KOTO restaurant in Hanoi, where the trainees tested their culinary skills on customers who easily accepted their smiling requests to be patient with their service. It was worth any wait as the food was delicious.

In my leisure time, I waited in a long line to see the embalmed body of Ho Chi Minh at the mausoleum in the centre of Ba Dinh Square. Sometimes I took part in t'ai chi exercises in parks, and people-watched at outdoor French cafés in wide, tree-lined streets, while simultaneously admiring gracious colonial French houses beside Oriental pagodas. I went to a cinema one evening; the film was the second of the vampire-themed *Twilight Saga*. I settled in a seat on its own close to the back. A sensible choice, as most of the audience continued to talk on their mobile phones, or to other patrons. The chatter later followed me onto the crowded streets to the night markets, where I was meeting a friend.

My sense of smell is acute in Asian cities and Hanoi was no exception. The alluring scents of what to expect on my dinner table were all around me. Pho noodle soup steamed temptingly on every corner as I walked through the street kitchens of the fourteenth-century quarter. My hunger increased at the potent aroma of bún chả – a dish of grilled pork and noodles thought to have originated in Hanoi. In fact, the whole experience was a treat for all my senses. Brightly painted ancient temples jostling for attention next to traditional craft villages. The vigorous entertainment on show in Ta Hien Street – dubbed the sleepless street – and much later the calm respite of Hoan Kiem lake nearby.

A weekend with Vietnamese students at famous tourist spot Halong Bay near the Chinese border was a stunning highlight. Halong, which means descending dragon, is 170 kilometres from Hanoi. Its more than 1,600 towering limestone islands and islets, caves, and traditional floating villages were declared a UNESCO World Heritage site in 1994. Visitors can take cruise tours that include on-board sleeping, head

Enjoying the famous UNESCO World Heritage site of Halong Bay, Vietnam, with students from the KOTO hospitality training school in Hanoi.

straight for Cat Ba Island for less visited but equally spectacular trips or go on a day tour in the bay as we did.

Our program debrief was in Sapa. It took eight hours by overnight train, 350 kilometres north-west from Hanoi, to reach this small mountain town. On seeing the glorious alpine landscape and inhaling the sweet air, I thought I was in Switzerland instead of about an hour's scooter ride from the Chinese border. Families from different ethnic groups wandered the quaint streets dressed in brilliant colours.

A Vietnamese colleague at KOTO told me before I left that Ho Chi Minh had always advocated the importance of lifelong work and education. Aspirations that have become even more vital for my well-being as I grow older.

3

Santiago, Ecuador and the Galapagos

I had been concerned for some time about single people in Australia being one of the most forgotten demographics in government policies. Particularly in light of a 2016 report by the Australian Bureau of Statistics which predicted a total of 3.2 million single households by 2041. I had noted that this expanding group's economic and societal needs were often skated over in federal budgets, compared to a traditional emphasis on support for families.

I lobbied major supermarkets to include small loaves of bread and meals for one with their usual family sizes. Their response of it being a limited market was proved wrong once they trialled the suggestion. My surveys exposed a big grievance – the travel supplement for a single room. So I created a plan for a tourist business for solo travel packages without a single-room supplement. Then competed in a best business idea contest for budding entrepreneurs. I didn't win, but was praised for 'showing entrepreneurial spirit'. I decided in November 2011 to brainstorm the ideas of global tourist operators attending a world travel conference in Ecuador's capital Quito. They would be well organised and versed in inventive travel. What also swayed my decision was a trip with them across the country after the conference, ending up at the Galapagos. Quito and Galapagos had been on my wish list for too long.

Santiago, Chile

In Santiago for a stopover on my way to Quito, I chatted to a British couple on my hotel terrace while feasting on a brunch of seafood-packed empanadas. They told me they were heading to – in their opinion – the essential two places to see in South America: Easter Island and the Galapagos. I didn't make it to the former, but found Santiago well worth a few days' exploration. Centro Gabriela Mistral is a tribute to Chilean poet Gabriela Mistral, the first Latin American woman to win the Nobel Prize in Literature. You can enjoy a regular concert there, check out the rotating art exhibits on the ground floor, and browse the little plazas, murals and cafés. The best views in Santiago were from the Parque Metropolitano, better known as Cerro San Cristóbal. At 722 hectares, the park with its swimming pools, a botanical garden and zoo is Santiago's largest green space.

A funicular takes you between different landscaped sections on one side, while the city's palm-lined Plaza de Armas contains the neoclassical cathedral and the National History Museum – where I met another traveller, an Australian woman, a university professor on sabbatical and near the end of her journeying across the continent. Peru was the best country, she said. What specially? Machu Picchu barely got a mention as she ticked them off. The Floating Islands of Lake Titicaca; a flight over the mysterious Nazca Lines – the UNESCO World Heritage site of a series of large ancient geoglyphs in the Nazca Desert – the Rainbow Mountains, their kaleidoscopic colours due to different environmental conditions and mineralogy. Vivid tourism images testified to their having been photoshopped into brilliance.

Ecuador

The trip across Ecuador was not exactly what I had hoped for. As the travellers were tour operators, it was not packaged for tourists with a reasonably strict itinerary, but it was flexible, as soon became obvious. The group often decided at the last minute where it wanted to go and did not always agree. Which is why we became stuck halfway up a steep track on the Avenue of the Volcanoes. In an area of one-way traffic, our driver swerved to avoid an oncoming truck, jammed into a pothole and teetered on the edge of a cliff. The 'we told you sos' echoed across the valley, as passengers slithered down the side of the vehicle and tried to breathe in the much higher altitude. Finally rescued, we arrived at our hotel very late. A decision was made to stick to some kind of schedule, more it seemed so as not to miss future dinners than to be better organised.

Travelling around the country to higher altitudes, I was occasionally offered coca tea, which has been claimed to help altitude sickness. Chewing coca leaves and drinking coca tea is common in the Andes, although its effectiveness is unproven. It is legal, but there is a chance the coca alkaloid content of coca may cause a postive drug test for cocaine. A 2010 study by Amitava Dasgupta, *Beating Drug Tests and Defending Positive Results: A Toxicologist's Perspective*, showed that drinking one cup of coca tea resulted in detectable concentrations of cocaine which can metabolise in the urine for at least twenty hours. Residual cocaine might still be present after de-cocainisation of coca leaves. Even coca teas that are supposedly free of cocaine may result in a positive drug test. I accepted the tea at one mountain stop without then knowing these facts. Despite less research, it seems reasonably safe to assume that if drinking coca tea can result in a positive drug test, then so too can chewing coca leaves.

A more successful excursion than our Avenue of Volcanoes adventure

Dancing with the locals from an Ecuadorian village at a railway station high in the Andes.

was the Devil's Nose train ride. It took us from the town of Alausi on a forty-five-minute journey to Silambe through impressive mountain scenery, in which time the train descended a heart-palpitating vertical kilometre. The community of the nearby village of Tolte greeted us at the destination. As the remainder of my group strolled around the handicraft and produce stalls or scrambled up the mountain trails, I danced on the platform with the villagers. When the train's horn beckoned me back, my dance partner asked me not to go. Meet his family, stay a while. I was tempted but didn't want to miss my few days on the Galapagos.

The Galapagos

Restricting tourist numbers is the only way Ecuador has been able to protect the flora, fauna and ecosystems of its famous Pacific archipelago which inspired Charles Darwin's theory of evolution. But nine years after I visited some of the thirteen major islands – there are six smaller islands, and scores of islets and rocks – the coronavirus pandemic struck and visitors stopped coming. A tourist-free Galapagos was unthinkable in 2011.

On a three-day cruise, we clambered early from our anchored ship into misty mornings onto small craft which dropped us at islands. I saw no straying tourists as our eagle-eyed guide kept us strictly to the allotted tracks. Hiking over the island of Española, the guide indicated colonies of blue-footed boobies whose names derived from a mispronunciation of their Spanish name *bobo*. They and the finches made famous in Darwin's evolutionary studies ignored the curious onlookers near them. Darwin's thirteen species of finches are endemic to the Galapagos. They evolved to have different beaks which are suited to varying food types such as large seeds or invertebrates. Darwin believed that animals become tame when they lived on remote, predator-free islands. They forgot how to fear, their ancestors having left the instinct of 'fight or flight' behind when they swam, flew or floated to escape prehistoric enemies on the mainland.

Highlights for me were seeing a seal giving birth, detecting a large land iguana shyly hiding in shrubbery, and colonies of black and orange marine iguanas, nearly camouflaged on slabs of black volcanic rock. These last are favourites with many biologists as only the Galapagos have a species of aquatic lizard that eats algae. A solitary albatross chick perching on its on-ground nest was my most poignant memory. The females don't lay eggs every year and the parents raise only one chick at a time. These large seabirds have been known to fly thousands of kilometres to find enough food for their offspring. I was reassured that some scientists and conservationists did provide food to nesting chicks left for long periods. So this one maybe had a good chance. But I still wondered if it survived.

4

Detours, reunions and closures

While I was wondering how to effectively use my masters degree, the university alerted me to a forthcoming symposium on transitional justice and conflict resolution in The Hague. I did not fit the normal profile of candidates – thirty-somethings with a legal background – but the intellectual opportunity was irresistible. I had two part-time jobs then, one as a journalist for an online newspaper and the other as a casual university teacher. As fewer international students were enrolling due to student visa changes and higher enrolment costs, casual work was being passed to full-time staff with falling workloads. When that job ended, I was ready to move on.

Coincidentally, I had just applied for a position as chief editor of the transitional justice website run by the Balkans Investigative Reporting Network (BIRN), despite having sparse knowledge of the topic. My degree had a unit on international law, but transitional justice – the notion of transitional democracy – was a stand-alone subject. I didn't get the job, but was accepted to the symposium. Once in the Netherlands, I could apply for similar positions at The Hague's many non-government organisations (NGOs) or at least use my love of international politics in some practical way. As the symposium did not start until August, I secured a teaching position at an international summer school in London two months before heading to The Hague and left Australia in May 2012.

Getting there was harder than expected. I had planned my route to take in five nights in Washington DC, a city I had wanted to visit for many years. As I prefer to not go on more than eleven-hour stretches between connections, I was toying with travelling via Auckland, then Hawaii (two nights), Los Angeles (one night) and Washington. Then a man I had become involved with when I first worked in Budapest in 2003 unexpectedly got in touch again before my South American visit. He lived in Wellington, New Zealand, and was now married. My relationship with him had been the first for a long time that I had considered might work long-term. When told of my pending trip to Europe and plan to fly from Auckland directly to the US, he asked if I could meet him in Wellington for a one- or two-day stopover. There were no direct flights from Wellington to the US but I decided to make the detour and fly to Auckland two days later.

He had never fully explained his reasons for leaving. I had met him in Vienna after what I thought was another temporary parting, believing our differences could be resolved. Instead, there was a harsh showdown in an outdoor café with no reason given for his decision, only that he considered it was best that we go in different directions. I never stopped believing he would come back; he did once but not in the way I had hoped. He emailed two years after the split. He wanted to return to Budapest to see me. After agreeing, his reply came weeks later. He said he had been in a happy, long-term relationship for some time. The next message was the worst cut: a photograph and short description of his wedding.

So why did I even want to see him again? Unfinished business? Closure or pure curiosity? I needed to know. He promised to meet me at the airport. On arrival, there was a message telling me he could only see me for breakfast the following morning and would meet me first at my hotel. I had hoped he wouldn't be so attractive to me after six years but he looked great – he'd been running in marathons, he said. The small talk faded as I asked about the reasons for hurtful situations. He spoke of his emotional immaturity then. It seemed like an easy excuse for unpredictable behaviour and experiences not learned. But it reminded me of times when I had ignored red flags, so determined had I been to make relationships work.

I asked if he had been playing egotistical games when he had last contacted me about meeting in Budapest. To ensure I still cared. He said he didn't know why, was sorry and had probably been weighing up what he might lose before taking the leap into marriage. In the end, explanations or lack of them did not matter so much as they had before. What was most important was that my strong feelings for him had gone. We promised to stay in touch, it started, then lapsed. But our good history remains intact in Budapest.

The detour via Wellington had a daunting effect on my travel itinerary. I arrived at the airport at six a.m. for my connections to Auckland and the US to find that fog had grounded all Auckland flights. I finally got there late that evening with limited time to board a flight to Los Angeles. But my relief was short-lived. Desperate at being squashed in a window seat next to an amorous couple for five hours in a full plane, I finally moved for the remaining six hours to a seat next to a very large man who had also coveted part of the seat I wanted.

After one night in Los Angeles, I was told my Washington reservation had been cancelled. The only cancellation I had made was for the Hawaii leg, and I had also made the date change on the DC route. I refused to leave the check-in counter until they found me a seat. Arriving exhausted in the US capital – I never sleep on planes – the remembered energy of the States from previous trips, and the cheeriness of the taxi driver as he took me to my hotel revived my expectancy of a new city. What followed were six delightful days where I was cossetted and slept and slept and rose to a heatwave and swimming, went to Georgetown and George Washington's home in Mount Vernon, and what Smithsonian museums I had time left to see.

My first European stop was Frankfurt for an overnight. The hotel, a short distance from the airport, had no restaurant so on the staff's advice – despite rain – I headed for an Italian place in a wooded area across the road. Finding it unappealing, I ventured further along the narrow forest path, savouring the nostalgic aroma of earth, damp leaves and woodsmoke redolent of spring in Europe. Hearing music, I spotted, hidden behind a grove of trees, a rustic *bierhaus* with a wood-panelled dining room. There, I ate the best vienna schnitzel accompanied by the music of a glockenspiel, harmonica and accordion. I was happy to be back and – despite the rigorous journey – very glad I had made the detour to Wellington.

5

The Hague, August 2012–March 2014

Attending the symposium not only whetted my appetite to know more about The Hague's global legal influence but also the vagaries of the city itself – a blend of new styles and old masters, royal palaces and only a short trip to bustling coastal towns like Scheveningen and its five-kilometre sandy beach. This region is a paradise for anglers – even Scheveningen's coat of arms features three herrings wearing gold crowns. From the beach, I was a North Sea boat ride away from my birth town near the Essex port of Harwich. A visit to the Hook of Holland had been a first trip abroad trip when growing up. I also went as a sixteen-year-old to the famous tulip gardens of Keukenhof in Lisse with a group of footballers from my local team, my then boyfriend being a player – a rowdy visit spent mostly in Rotterdam. In the early 1990s, my posting to the Australian Embassy in Brussels took me on regular trips to the Dutch publishing company near Utrecht which printed pocket books on Australia.

I had always known the country as Holland, but it had an official name change to the Netherlands in January 2020. North and South Holland are actually two of the twelve provinces of the country. The Dutch government believes the name change will encourage tourists to explore further than the major cities of Amsterdam and The Hague, shifting the international focus from certain aspects of national life such as its recreational drug culture and the red-light district.

6

The Peace Palace

In 1998, former UN Secretary-General Boutros Boutros-Ghali described The Hague as 'the legal capital of the world'. But does the Netherlands seat of government live up to the title? I had the chance to find out when commissioned by *The International Correspondent* to write an article marking the Peace Palace centenary in 2013. This beautiful Neo-Renaissance style building houses the International Court of Justice, the Permanent Court of Arbitration, the Hague Academy of International Law and the Peace Palace Library.

Its benefits are definitely worth the costs according to Dr Guido Acquaviva. I had interviewed Dr Acquaviva when he was senior legal officer and *chef de cabinet* to the office of the president at the Special Tribunal for Lebanon and for six years legal officer for the International Criminal Tribunal for the Former Yugoslavia (ICTY). He firmly dismissed any charge that investing in international courts and tribunals to promote international peace and justice was akin to squandering money when compared with the costs of one stealth bomber or nuclear missile. The legal process in the actual country where the crimes were allegedly committed was no quicker than that conducted in The Hague, he said.

Dr Acquaviva told me the atmosphere in the courts was similar to that depicted in some American movies, with cross-examination by lawyers but no jury. Only professional judges decided the verdict, made more complicated first by language barriers and simultaneous interpretation. The trials were very different from continental European ones.

The Peace Palace. The Neo-Renaissance landmark in The Hague houses the International Court of Justice, the Permanent Court of Arbitration, The Hague Academy of International Law and the Peace Palace Library.

'The beauty of this job is that you get the perspectives of legal professionals from all over the world,' he said.

My group from the symposium attended a trial at the ICTY of an alleged war criminal. It was very slow because of translations. Difficult too to sense the atmosphere or even the demeanours of the defendant and legal team as we watched through a thick screen in the public gallery, headphones firmly clamped. Several errant whisperers were ejected without caution.

The defendant was not as well known as the one in the final ICTY trial in November 2017. Charged with alleged war crimes then was Bosnian-Serbian general, Ratko Mladic, who was widely believed to have masterminded the Srebrenica massacre in July 1995, killing more than 8,000 Bosniaks, mainly men and boys. Mladic was sentenced to life imprisonment. The subsequent appeal was to be handled by the Mechanism for International Criminal Tribunals as the case was unfinished by the ICTY before its closure at the end of 2017. After being delayed twice, the verdict was delivered on Tuesday, 8 June 2021. Mladic lost his final appeal against his convictions for genocide, war crime and crimes against humanity and will spend the remainder of his life in prison.

7

Macedonia and its new name

A day after the symposium ended, I flew to the former Yugoslav Republic of Macedonia (FYROM), known officially since 2018 as the Republic of North Macedonia or North Macedonia. I was attending a week-long workshop there on investigative journalism in countries with media censorship. The BIRN network running the event had in 2011 rejected me for a chief editor's position. I hoped to persuade them I was now worth employing on the strength of my transitional justice studies.

Greece had long opposed the name of Macedonia because of its own region of the same name. The naming dispute was officially settled when the leaders of both countries ratified the Prespa Agreement, so-called after the lake whose shores hosted the signing ceremony. The name, North Macedonia, was agreed as a compromise to Greek fears that its northern neighbour had territorial designs upon its north-western province. The people of North Macedonia have still retained the right to refer to themselves and their language as Macedonian.

But the truth of Alexander the Great's legacy remains a mystery to me, despite evidence that Greece has the rightful claim. For example, historians in North Macedonia point to artefacts and ancient records as well as several forts built by the military genius on land that today belongs to North Macedonia. Tens of thousands of coins of Macedonian kings are also said to be spread over the country's territory.

My stay in the capital Skopje was brief as I was heading by bus the next morning to the media event, two hours into the mountains. A huge statue of a warrior on horseback, cast in the popular image of Alexander the Great, dominated the main square. Other statues, rising out of spotlit fountains, appeared to show the conqueror's father and mother. Statues of emperors, politicians, poets, lions, and horses cast imposing shadows either side of the Vardar River. After belonging to many empires, including Roman, Byzantine, Ottoman, and Yugoslavian, most of its buildings were rebuilt after being destroyed in a massive 1963 earthquake. Skopje has long been shared by Christians and Muslims, who still come together at the fascinating Old Bazaar, one of the Balkans' largest markets. The bazaars were a central feature of life in many Ottoman era cities.

And yes, I did meet my potential employers. I updated them on my fresh qualifications and they offered editing work, but it was a casual position replacing staff on summer holidays, so short-lived. It was worth a try, if only for a glimpse at a new country, now with a new name.

8

Art and philosophy on my doorstep

I found a rental apartment in The Hague before this trip, planning to seek work on my return. It was in a canal house in the Dunne Bierkade. At the end of my street there was a choice of Chinatown's fare one way, and Nepalese, Eritrean and other more exotic cuisine on the other. My studio apartment, painted in various shades of red, was a spacious, light-filled kitchenette, bedroom, and separate shower and toilet. Dominating the room was a large photograph of Audrey Hepburn similar to ones I had seen in other apartments. Hepburn's mother, Baroness Ella van Heemstra, was from a long line of Dutch nobility dating back to the twelfth century. She had always wanted to be an actress and encouraged her daughter to achieve her unfulfilled dream. It is said that Hepburn had to eat tulip bulbs to survive during wartime in the Netherlands. She also spoke in interviews about her teenage years raising money for the Dutch Resistance by designing dances and performing at underground concerts.

I was unaware when I began living in Dunne Bierkade that my apartment was very close to where the Dutch masters of the Golden Age had lived – a period from 1581 to 1672 when Dutch trade, science, military, and art were among the most acclaimed in the world. The seventeenth-century philosopher Baruch (later Benedictus) Spinoza also had a home around the corner from mine. City architect and director of town planning Claes Dircx van Balckeneynde built a house in the neigbourhood. Van Balckeneynde was known for his boarded-up wooden ceilings. Protruding beams became a thing of the past thanks to his designs (the name Balckeneynde means beams' end). He oversaw the construction of the palaces of the family of Orange, and what is now the official residence of the prime minister of the Netherlands, the Cats House. It was originally built for prominent poet and politician Jacob Cats, who lived there from 1652 till his death eight years later.

My former landlords, Fundatie Voorhoeve, own the houses once occupied by three famous painters. They were landscape painter Jan van Goyen; his son-in-law Jan Steen, whose forte was interiors, acclaimed for their psychological insight, sense of humour and lavish colours; and Paulus Potter, celebrated chiefly for his paintings of animals in landscapes. The Outdoor Museum, Dunne Bierkade 17, arranges tours to the houses. I regularly attended dinners hosted by my landlords at Van Goyen's former home, where Steen had also worked. Seated at long trestle tables with the other guests —mostly tenants or short-term visitors – we ate in the rustic dining room watched over by Van Goyen's famous paintings, such as his 1647 *The Hague from the North West*, a view across farmlands and windmills to the distinctive spires of the Great or St James Church founded in the late thirteenth century, probably as a wooden church. The present church was built in stages between the fourteenth and sixteenth centuries.

Dutch post-impressionist painter Vincent van Gogh first lived for six years as an art dealer in one of Dunne Bierkade's small courtyards. He began his art lessons with the nineteenth-century painters of De Haagse School, which played a crucial role in his evolution as an artist. Van Gogh's first letters to his brother Theo, his first paintings, his first use of artistic aids such as the perspective frame and his first paid commission, all originated during his time in The Hague. It is still possible to follow Van Gogh's footsteps through the city and its surrounding areas. The Van Gogh Experience organises an exhibition of his art in the immediate vicinity (no original works) and offers sightseeing tours.

9

Tulipmania

The Turkish word for a turban seems to have been used for the tulip in western European languages because a fully opened tulip was purported to resemble the headwear. The Turks first cultivated the flowers as early as AD 1000. Tulipmania in Turkey struck in the sixteenth century at the time of the Ottoman Empire, when the Sultan demanded cultivation of particular blooms for his pleasure.

After the flowers were introduced into Holland in the late sixteenth century, the tulip craze erupted and contract prices for some bulbs reached extraordinarily high levels. Homes, estates and industries were mortgaged so that bulbs could be bought for resale at higher prices.

Before 1633, Holland's tulip trade had been restricted to professional growers and experts, but the steadily rising prices tempted many middle-class and poor families to speculate in the market. Its dramatic crash in February 1637 was triggered by doubts that prices would never fall. A large part of this rapid decline was driven by the fact that people had purchased bulbs on credit, hoping to repay their loans when they sold their bulbs for profit. But once prices started their decline, holders were forced to liquidate – to sell their bulbs at any price and to declare bankruptcy in the process. Barterers for the precious bulbs plumbed their creativity. A bed, a complete wardrobe of clothes, and a thousand pounds of cheese were some of the offerings. At the height of the mania, the bulbs were regarded as too valuable to risk planting by their formerly wealthy purchasers, and it became popular to display the plain ungrown bulbs. Apparently, a plan to protect them backfired when a visiting sailor mistook one for an onion and ate it for breakfast. Yet almost overnight, fortunes were swept away, creating financial ruin for many ordinary Dutch families. This was all revealed to me in Amsterdam's Tulip Museum, whose unimposing facade I discovered by chance while wandering along Prinsengracht and finding it at number 16.

Jan van Goyen was one of the wealthier speculators of tulip bulbs who suffered severe losses when the market collapsed. He had also supported his family working as an auctioneer, an appraiser of art and a real-estate investor. The last restored some of his finances. One major project was organising the building of Baruch Spinoza's house. The philosopher lived at Paviljoensgracht 72–74 from 1670 for seven years. His acclaimed book *Ethica* was published posthumously in 1677. Spinoza's work as a lens grinder meant that he was constantly inhaling small particles of glass, which may have contributed to the lung disease he died from at forty-four.

10

Baruch Spinoza

It intrigues me that certain questions discussed in both religion and philosophy tend to be very much alike. Both wrestle with problems like what is the nature of reality? Why are we here and what should we be doing? What is really most important in life? More than three centuries ago, Spinoza grappled with these and many other questions still very relevant today: the relationship between church and state, citizens and politics, power and freedom. As a political thinker, he believed that the power of the state should never be entrusted to a single person because it would be abused. As a rationalist, he was credited with having laid the foundation for the eighteenth-century Enlightenment.

In *Ethica*, Spinoza argued that as the chain of cause and effect was inescapable the future was already set. He presented an alternate spiritual view of God/Nature as a whole system of which humans are a part. One consequence of this was that everything that happened in nature, and everything that nature's lawful order handed out to us personally, was necessary; in the same way that the conclusion of a logical or mathematical demonstration was necessary.

Spinoza's unorthodox ideas have been claimed to be the reasons in 1656 that he was formally excommunicated by the synagogue in Amsterdam at the age of twenty-three. Many scholars have contradicted this explanation as it rarely took into account that, at the time, the Jewish community there was very broad-minded. Its social and political leaders (the parnassim) were businessmen rather than rabbis. There must have been deeper reasons for this drastic decision which have never been fully clarified.

Spinoza moved from Amsterdam to the coastal town of Rijnsburg

The Spinoza house in Rijnsburg, the Netherlands, now a museum, includes more than 300 works dating from the seventeenth and eighteenth centuries by and on the Dutch philosopher.

in 1661. Most traditional accounts assume that he had tired of his enforced isolation – including from his family – or that he wanted a peaceful place to pursue his philosophical work. However, Spinoza himself reported that someone had tried to kill him with a knife as he was leaving a theatre. For the rest of his life, he kept the coat he had been wearing, torn by the knife.

In December 2018, a friend and I visited the Spinoza house in Rijnsburg. It's not easy to find as it nestles incongruously in suburbia, a statue of the philosopher in its small garden, backing on to modern houses. The volunteer guide showed us Spinoza's collection of 161 books, describing how they were all hidden in a German salt mine in the Second World War and returned in perfect condition when the war ended. The house includes a working replica of Spinoza's lens grinding equipment, and a copy of the visitor's book which Albert Einstein signed on 2 November 1920. Einstein was most influenced by Spinoza's thesis of an unrestricted determinism and the belief in a superior intelligence revealed in the harmony and beauty of nature. His visit inspired the scientist to write a poem about the philosopher.

> How much do I love that noble man
> More than I could tell with words
> I fear though he'll remain alone
> With a holy halo of his own.

The house is at Spinozalaan 29, 2231 SG Rijnsburg, a thirty-minute bus ride from Leiden train station.

Researching Spinoza's life and work prompted me to think more deeply about my own beliefs.

11

Religion, nature and spirituality

The lines between religion and spirituality are not clear and distinct, but rather points on belief systems known as religion. As an agnostic, I interpret spirituality as a personal and private view of what may or may not exist, while religion tends to incorporate public rituals and organised doctrines which I avoid. However, I do hold certain beliefs based on inexplicable experiences which have challenged my agnosticism.

On the Greek island of Patmos, I felt unexpectedly elated while seated in the cave where St John is reputed to have written the Book of Revelation. Designated as 'Holy Island' by the Greek parliament in 1981 as well as a World Heritage site by UNESCO in 1999, Patmos had been used as a place of exile by the Romans on account of its steep morphology. That's how St John, exiled by the Emperor Domitian, found safe refuge there in the first century AD.

On another occasion, I described an unaccountable event at a series of discussions on evolution versus creationism at the home of the pastor of the English Reformed Church in Amsterdam. Some in the group spoke of knowing about this phenomenon. The pastor said he wished for such an experience.

I spoke of a time eighteen months after my husband's sudden death when I had been sick with influenza for a week. A knock on my door woke me early one morning. A courier stood there with a large bouquet of flowers from my mother. The card said, 'For Ron's birthday'. It was 18 July. My late husband would have been fifty-six. Within a short time, I was in my car and driving to Binalong, the village an hour from Canberra where I owned a former inn built in 1851. Once frequented by bushrangers and supposedly haunted, we had treated the place more as a weekender and both loved it. Ron's grave is at Binalong Cemetery. It was a shining day as I sped along country roads, spirits sky high. I only stopped for an injured bird huddled on the road, but was unable to save it.

The journey and the two days I stayed in the village were enhanced by a glow I can only describe as an aura. Not, I believe, a reflection of my state of being, but the energy field of other living things; trees, flowers, streams, animals. Enveloping me in a complete sense of belonging. The pleasure of seeing people I had avoided since his death. The lack of emotional pain. The belief that I would be able to always return there with no debilitating sense of loss. My grief had broken.

Then the exuberance dipped. Hoping to recover its intensity, I walked on ground comfortingly familiar when my world was so different. Along a winding forested path above the house, past the white froth of hawthorn hedges, across paddocks, almost deafened by the relentless clicking and buzzing of cicadas. The insects 'sing' as a way to communicate, reproduce and maybe even defend themselves. One I almost trod on was lying on its back, legs waving frantically. I tried to turn it over, but a wing was broken. How do you mend an insect's wing? I had read somewhere that some cicadas have shrivelled-up or damaged wings which can happen while moulting and their wings and body are still soft. I mused wryly that we had a broken wing in common. Mine would mend with deep scars. This creature's would not.

I eventually sold the house after months of failing to let go and rarely returned to the village. The last time I went in 2016, the new owner showed me how well the old place was thriving in her care. A heady form of closure took hold of me. That universe radiance happened on a few other occasions, but never with the same magnitude. The experience could perhaps be explained by the ideas presented in a book, *Health Promotion Strategies Through the Lifespan*, by nurses Ruth Beckmann Murray and Judith Proctor Zentner. They wrote, 'The spiritual dimension tries to be in harmony with the universe, and strives for answers about the infinite. It comes into focus when the person faces emotional stress, physical illness, or death.' I remember this experience as a signal of hope which supported me when I needed it most. A closed curtain had begun to part. Showing what could be possible. Rupturing doubt and disputing disbelief. Then closing again.

My affinity with nature is especially strong in ancient lands like Australia, particularly so when I worked for the former Australian National Parks and Wildlife Service. On assignment in the country's enigmatic heart where the immense monolith of Uluru and the rock domes of Kata Tjuta dominate the Uluru-Kata Tjuta National Park, I learned how significant this world heritage place was as the Tjurkurpa (traditional law) of the Anangu people. They lease the land to the Australian government and work in partnership with Parks Australia to manage the area.

Determined to explore this vast nation, I sometimes had to face phobias. One instance when employed by the Australian Customs Service stands out. I flew in a three-seater Nomad aircraft from Darwin to Groote Eylandt, the biggest island in the Gulf of Carpentaria. I sat behind the pilot and a photographer, my hand in my jacket pocket clutching a small flask of brandy. I had not told them about my fear of small aircraft. I once flew in a small plane from Paraburdoo in Western Australia to Perth with violent turbulence the whole way. I was convinced it would crash. My anxiety about flying was exacerbated in 1988 when, as a front-seat passenger, I was involved in a near fatal car crash in Canberra. I prefer to drive a car rather than be the passenger so I am in control. Becoming a pilot might have helped, but moving to Europe and train travel was a better option.

Not far out of Darwin, the pilot of the Nomad suddenly dived down over Kakadu national park towards Jim Jim Falls. 'Aren't they wonderful?' he yelled.

'There's hardly any water. Get back up now,' I shouted.

'Don't like flying, Lyn? We have two engines if one fails.' He turned to grin as I swigged my brandy and mumbled something profane about crazy pilots.

Returning relatively smoothly back to Darwin two days later, I concentrated on the glorious sunset and almost relaxed. Not long after, the Nomad was permanently grounded, reportedly because of ongoing technical problems.

The longer my career took me to far-flung parts of the country and to positions overseas, the more I understood why Australian poet Dorothea Mackellar's poem 'My Country' is so popular with homesick Australians. The second stanza is possibly one of the most well known and recited pieces of poetry in Australian history.

> I love a sunburnt country
> A land of sweeping plains
> Of ragged mountain ranges
> Of droughts and flooding rains
> I love her far horizons
> I love her jewel sea
> Her beauty and her terror
> The wide brown land for me.

Mackellar started to write the poem in 1904, when she was nineteen, while visiting England and missing her home country. Living on foreign soils, I too have missed a sky such a vivid blue it engulfs my sight after years in softer climates. The vast sense of distance constantly beckons. Landscapes stained in ochres, russets; purple-reds of rocks and gorges and dried river beds. Blue sky on blue sea on green palms of the northern tropics; into the external territories like Christmas Island, where huge land crabs climbed trees, blocked my path through the forest as they feasted on the mulch, or halted to wave curious pincers. Places of incandescent colour, light and energy that permanently tethered my spirit to this unpredictable, unforgiving country that Mackellar described.

12

My French farce, March 2014

I found media jobs in NGOs in The Hague but the contracts were short for paid work as many employers preferred to employ interns without paying them. In some places I worked, they were rarely praised for their dedication. Funding for NGOs was also tight as accountability to donors became a much greater key to retaining their worth. Not wishing to join the ever growing band of volunteers giving the city a name for being the centre of volunteerism, I moved to Aix-en-Provence, France, in March 2014 to upgrade my French, only to return to the Netherlands three months later to take up a fixed contract as a media relations specialist with Greenpeace International in Amsterdam.

The language school I chose placed me with a host family who spoke only French. An American student of French was also living there. At dinner, I followed the rapid conversation with difficulty. The American seemed quite fluent.

I asked her, in English, at the end of the lengthy meal, if she could show me how to use the washing machine, which was workable but had apparently developed a fault.

Silence.

Then, 'Don't speak to me in English.'

Two days later, my language school called to tell me the hosts wanted me to leave. It appeared the American had complained to her school that English was being spoken, violating the rules of her contract with the hosts. As she had signed for a six-month renewable stay, I was out. My school had led the hosts to believe my French was of a much higher standard.

My next hosts were a husband and wife, she dominating, he gentle and quietly spoken. My bedroom was colour-schemed in different shades of orange, but surprisingly restful at first. It soon became clear my life there was to be far from relaxed and was closely monitored. I began eating breakfast one morning, then got up to get something from the kitchen. When I returned, the dishes and my barely eaten food had been cleared away. I was chastised for leaving a few crumbs on the table and not making the bed correctly.

Nerves frazzled after two weeks, I found a studio apartment to rent. I told my hosts I would move when my time was up with them in three weeks. Madame at first agreed then told me to leave immediately. I could not understand her shouted explanation. I was on the street again. After a night in a hotel, I moved into the apartment earlier than planned after a French friend negotiated with my landlady, who lived in a remote village. Still determined to make the move work, I left the language school and continued my studies with university students I befriended and who I paid.

My new home was off Boulevard de Republique, one of the main spines leading from the Cours Mirabeau, a café-lined street cutting through the centre of the university city. My street curved around wisteria-covered walls, and blue shuttered amber-hued buildings. The tantalising drift of fresh baguettes and pastries from the nearby bakery daily lured me up early for breakfast. I soon learned to honour the obligatory two-hour or more lunch after a hot arrival at a swimming pool one unusually warm day and finding it closed from noon to three – a lucrative period I would have thought for workers seeking lunchtime swims.

Provence villages are said to be among the loveliest in France. My favourite was Roussillon in the Luberon region in the heart of one of the biggest ochre deposits in the world. Famous for its magnificent red cliffs and ochre quarries. the red, yellow and brown shades of the earth contrasting strikingly with the lush green pine trees. However, Aix-en-Provence is a tough town according to a French author I met there. It took him eighteen months to adjust and he was reluctant to explain why. He said my time there would show me.

I talked in English with a public relations staffer giving out tourist brochures at the railway station. The same person was there to sell me train tickets a week later. When I started to tell her what I wanted, she told me in French she didn't speak English. I reminded her of our previous encounter and she handed me my ticket without answering. The receptionist at the library said I should speak French to him. I had tried *parlez vous Anglais* first just in case. I explained that I had just arrived to improve my French and wondered how other foreigners on short trips managed without the language. A prospective employer who had agreed to create a teaching position for me at his university after we had discussed its value, instead offered the job to someone else – and 'forgot' to tell me. I knew this could happen anywhere, but even the French told me that deep friendships were more easily forged in northern France, while southerners were often shallow with their feelings. The reverse of course could be true. It reminded me of an earlier time in Hamburg when I was told not to go to the south, especially Munich, as the residents were dour. Presumably they all perked up at Oktoberfest.

Undeterred, I joined the French-speaking social group *On Va Sortir* (Let's Go Out). I managed the general introductions but dried up in more complex discussions. I met expats searching for the dream, and finding a nightmare, as some told me. They complained about the bureaucracy, the concentrated efforts to make things as hard as possible to run businesses or live comfortably.

I spent some time talking to a Normandy girl who had spent several months in Australia as a working student, She said she loved the feeling there that anything is possible but also not to worry too much about study, just have a good time. All right when you are twenty and want to surf and jam but I wanted a rewarding project to get my teeth into.

I had signed a three-month lease for my apartment but to get the internet connected, I needed a permanent address and French bank account. National banks wouldn't accept me with the short lease so I approached the only international bank, hoping for more flexible rules. The teller or whoever it was regarded me with suspicion when I asked about opening an account, and wanted to know what savings and assets I had. Customers had to have a certain high amount before being signed up. The manager I requested to speak to confirmed haughtily that I did not meet the criteria for assets.

I became a tourist again. An hour's drive to Avignon to see the bridge made famous in the song. The medieval Pont Saint-Bénézet, also known as the Pont d'Avignon, is a world heritage site built over the River Rhône in the twelfth century. It lasted until 1688, when it was almost destroyed by a devastating flood, leaving four arches of its original twenty-two.

The song which I remembered singing in my French classes at school is misleading as the lyrics suggest that people used to dance on the bridge – *Sur le pont d'Avignon l'on y danse tout en rond* (On the

Sur le pont d'Avignon. The bridge, a world heritage site, was almost destroyed by fire in 1688, leaving four arches of its original twenty-two.

bridge of Avignon, people dance in a ring). However, the bridge was only wide enough for a cart to pass. Today, it is believed that people used to dance on the islands in the Rhône under the arches. The 'dancing on the bridge' form of the song that we know today seems to have been sung only after the original bridge was washed away in the seventeenth-century flood. It is probably more an idea than fact. Or the words *sous* (under) and *sur* (on) changed unacknowledged over the centuries. Close to the bridge, the huge fourteenth-century Gothic architecture of the Palais des Papes (Palace of Popes) took my breath away.

Then a day in Marseilles, thirty minutes on the bus from Aix. I shook off the claustrophobia in this smaller city. Marseilles port greeted me with life and colour. People everywhere. Buskers, strollers, shouting and laughing. The old areas, shabby and run-down, shadowed with the mafia, violence, crime. All these things I was warned happened there. But it brimmed with vitality. The sea was near; don't stay late at night; watch your bag. I got the train back to Aix and wanted to go again.

I had been further south in the past to Nice, Monte Carlo, Monaco, St Tropez, Cannes; did my French language training in Nice before taking up the diplomatic post in Brussels. Looked further this time along the coast from Marseilles and found quaint villages with marinas tucked under bridges. Cafés, art galleries painted in gelato colours, in their own compact valley. So the city turned into a captivating lilliputian world. The sixteen-kilometre stretch of coast between Cassis and Marseilles featured not only France's highest sea cliffs, but also a series of *calanques*, fjord-like inlets carved into the white limestone. The best time for walking around Cassis is the beginning of June or the end of September, when mornings are crisper and evenings mild.

Friends live in Sanary-sur-Mer, a charming port in coastal Provence on the Mediterranean, about fifty kilometres south of Marseilles. Sanary is a microcosm of what you expect to see in the south of France. A dazzle of bougainvillea, oleanders, artists' palette houses and apartments. That hurting sun. 'Oh, not another warm sunny day,' my friends sometimes groan.

What happened to the stirring aromas of the seasons in those hot places I have lived? Something primitive, almost feral seeping through the earth. Constant sun is not good for my soul, neither are relentless damp, grey days. Where to find the balance?

There were special times in France. A concert one balmy night in Aix town centre with new friend, Annie. Tambourine players, drums and whistles and even a singing of the Provence national anthem. Then to her apartment, a tasteful two-bedroom she bought fifteen years ago. Its back and front gardens fragrant with the flowers of Provence – white, pink and yellow peonies, lavender and red poppies. I invited her to dinner with my Dutch visitors who were arriving at the weekend.

13

Cézanne and Mont Sainte-Victoire

The most famous resident of Aix-en-Provence was undoubtedly artist Paul Cézanne. Credited with forming the bridge between late nineteenth-century Impressionism and early twentieth-century Cubism, Cézanne was described by both Matisse and Picasso as 'the father of us all'. He introduced two basic tenets widely acknowledged as the foundations of Modernism. The first was based on his use of geometry: he built his compositions not with lines, but rather with volumetric planes of colour, fracturing images into distinct parts. The second was achieved by limiting his use of colour. He created built compositions by letting the paper or canvas stand for solid forms, as seen in his work *La Montagne Sainte-Victoire*, 1905–6. The mountain overlooking his birthplace dominated many of his paintings of Provence from 1886.

'Treat nature by means of the cylinder, the sphere, the cone, everything brought into proper perspective,' Cézanne wrote in 1904, two years before his death. 'The landscape becomes a thinking, living being within me. I become one with my picture.' He found geologic forces trapped in the rocks. Powerful saps coursing through the trees.

I felt an uncanny frisson the first time I saw the mountain. The wide limestone massif has a symbolic appeal in the region, being linked to an ancient Roman victory and several early Christian festivals. Cézanne once said of Aix-en-Provence, 'When you're born here, nothing else is good enough.' Did he also mean that the mountain always enticed him back? This may sound far-fetched but I have experienced how places can take hold.

Once when working in Central Australia, I stayed briefly with the family of the chief ranger of the Australian National Parks and Wildlife Service. He rarely took holidays after years living within sight of Uluru. Some of his former colleagues told me that he would often return early from holidays. Maybe drawn back to the only place he needed – and which he believed needed him.

My reaction bordering on recognition when seeing Mont Sainte-Victoire was very different from the recoil I felt faced with the craggy volcanic peaks of the Glass House Mountains towering above the surrounding Sunshine Coast in Queensland and named in 1770 by Lieutenant James Cook. He wrote, 'These hills lie but a little way inland, and not from each other. They are remarkable for the singular form of their elevation, which very much resembles a glass house, and for this reason I called them Glass Houses.' The glass houses he referred to were the glass making foundries in Yorkshire, England, which reminded him of a familiar landscape.

I could not understand why they oppressed me so much, especially the highest Mount Beerwah at 556 metres above sea level, and the most identifiable, Mount Tibrogargan. From certain angles the latter resembles a face staring east towards the Pacific Ocean. Maybe it is because their strange shapes loom out threateningly from a flat landscape. Or the bleak Aboriginal legends about them. Or the many climbers who have died. All of these or none but that mystifying feeling. Nature in a guise and size overwhelming to a tiny human.

Conradian landscapes. The Polish-British writer Joseph Conrad wrote of nature's brutal forces in classics like his fictionalised account of colonial Africa, *Heart of Darkness*. Landscapes devoid of 'that spiritual essence which permeates and redeems the transfixed face of nature in romantic symbolist representations'. The book's protagonist Marlow considers nature to be truly resilient. That its power will not be fully taken over. Biding its time and returning only after humanity thinks it has conquered it.

Mont Sainte-Victoire obviously exerted a power over Cézanne. Its distinctive silhouette greeted him every day when he was at the family home at Le Jas de Bouffan. One of his favourite views of the mountain was from the abandoned sandstone Bibemus quarries. There you can see slabs of saffron-coloured rock intermixed with the rich greens of pine and olive trees. Nearby is the small cottage he rented to store his painting supplies. The Painters Park, one of four sites on the Cézanne trail, is a kilometre climb north of the painting studio (Atelier Cézanne). The best time to visit is an hour before sunset when the colours change and intertwine on the mountainside.

14

Van Gogh in Arles

I had not been a great fan of Vincent van Gogh's paintings until I lived in the Netherlands and France – the countries which so defined his craft. One of the revelations for me was the effect that Japanese art had on him. He was introduced to Impressionism when he moved to Paris in 1886 but also explored Japonism, a French term first used by Jules Claretie in his book *L'Art Francais en 1872*. Van Gogh admired Japonism's bold designs. Flat areas of pure colour and elegant and simple lines. He moved from Paris to Arles, Provence, in 1888 to find the brilliance and light that would wash out detail and simplify forms, reducing the world around him to the sort of pattern he admired in Japanese woodblocks. He even described Arles once as the Japan of the south.

Arles is fascinating and not only for its famous resident. UNESCO inscribed its Roman and Romanesque monuments on its World Heritage list. An arena dating to the first century BCE that seated more than 20,000 spectators was still being used for bullfights and plays when I visited in 2014. Excavations at a Roman theatre had retrieved many art objects, including the *Venus of Arles* now in the Louvre, Paris.

After moving into the Yellow House in the centre of Arles, Van Gogh wrote in a letter to his sister Wilhelmina, 'My house here is painted the yellow colour of fresh butter on the outside with glaringly green shutters; it stands in the full sunlight in a square which has a green garden with plane trees, oleanders and acacias. It is completely whitewashed inside, and the floor is made of red bricks. And over it is the intensely blue sky. In this I can live and breathe, meditate and paint.'

He completed 200 paintings and more than 100 drawings and watercolours in his fifteen months in Arles.

Panels mark the places in Arles where Van Gogh set up his easel. They include Place Lamartine, where the Yellow House once stood before being bombed in the Second World War; the Place du Forum for the *Café in the Evening*; the Trinquetaille bridge for the *Staircase of the Trinquetaille Bridge*; and the Rhone River embankment for *Starry Night over the Rhône*. My guide in Arles believed *Starry Night* had a pall of loneliness over it which characterised the painter. An observation which ran counter to the prolific two years Van Gogh spent at his brother Theo's Montmartre home. There he made many friends including the French post-impressionist Paul Gauguin, who later joined him at the Yellow House.

Records show that Van Gogh suffered a psychotic episode in Arles in which he was claimed to have cut off part of his ear and given it to a prostitute. An alternative story was that Gauguin, an expert fencer, had cut it off with a sword in the middle of a fight. In the 2009 book *Van Gogh's Ear: Paul Gauguin and the Pact of Silence*, Hamburg-based academics Hans Kaufmann and Rita Wildegans argued that the official version of events, based largely on Gauguin's accounts, contained inconsistencies and that both artists suggested that the truth was more complex. While curators at the Van Gogh Museum in Amsterdam stand by the theory of self-mutilation, Kaufmann said Van Gogh dropped hints in letters to Theo, once commenting, 'Luckily Gauguin is not yet armed with machine guns and other dangerous war weapons.'

At the Arles hospital, I saw copies of paintings Van Gogh had done as a patient there after the ear incident. But when I later asked an art historian at the Van Gogh Museum why his time in Arles was not featured at an exhibition on his life it was showing, she denied he had lived there. Rather, she insisted he was only in Saint-Rémy-de-Provence in an asylum for the mentally ill and later in Auvers-sur-Oise near Paris, where he remained until his death on 29 July 1890, aged thirty-seven. She also discounted a long-held theory that he was murdered because, she implied, suicide was the most publicly accepted story. The museum gave a similar answer to the Pulitzer Prize-winning authors Steven Naifeh and Gregory White Smith, authors of *Van Gogh: the Life*. In it they alleged the artist had been shot, possibly accidentally, by two boys.

Coincidentally, while writing this I discovered that a biographical drama about the artist's final years was showing at my local cinema. Entitled *At Eternity's Gate*, it supported Naifeh's and Smith's controversial theory. The film deeply affected me as it showed the hidden depths of the man behind the 'tormented' public image, interpreting his work in a way I finally could understand. What he took from Impressionism was the freedom to paint the colours he wanted. He painted furiously for days, applying paint in bold colours that made his canvases seem like pottery, Gauguin's character says in the film.

To present this authentic image, American director Julian Schnabel adapted the screenplay from hundreds of letters Van Gogh wrote to Theo. In them, he spoke of using his passion for painting as a restorative drug for bouts of depression, about being addicted to beauty, in love with the transcendence of nature, which he considered holy. Rich with description he writes, 'I see a flat landscape. I see nothing but eternity, am I the only one who sees it?'

Nineteenth-century French art critic and painter Albert Aurier described Van Gogh as the only painter he knew 'who perceives the colouration of things with such intensity, with such a metallic, gem-like quality'. Aurier's view that Van Gogh was an artist of the future was reflected in the film. It suggested that one of the reasons he had left the earth too early was his need to see the world to come. The world of the senses.

15

Amsterdam, June 2014–October 2015

I had expected to continue improving my French long enough to sit the state exam. But two months after arriving in Aix, Greenpeace International offered me a six-month contract as a media specialist at its headquarters in Amsterdam. Greenpeace accommodated me in its house for the first month while I searched for a place to live. I enjoyed the comings and goings of other boarders like Pablo, who arrived from Spain on a temporary transfer. A captain on one of the Greenpeace boats, he was excitable, fun, a lively dynamic in what was then a quieter household. We all watched the soccer World Cup at various pubs, and often took turns at cooking our favourite national dishes. His were Spanish pancakes, or *filloas*, traditionally from the north of Spain, similar to French crêpes but thinner. A British housemate made sausages and mash. I cooked roast lamb, an English and Australian favourite.

My next move was to a shared house with a cosy room and view overlooking a busy canal. On Gay Pride day and the King's Day national holiday, the canal echoed all night with frivolity, horns blowing, loud music and dancing to the extent I thought the smaller craft would sink. Revellers were allowed to throw fireworks indiscriminately in the streets at the festivals and on New Year's Eve, with accidents aplenty. If you have ever watched the Dutch national soccer team play football anywhere in the world or been in Amsterdam during King's Day (formerly Queen's Day), you may have wondered why nearly all Dutch people are wearing orange. Simply, orange is the colour of the Dutch royal family, which hails from the House of Orange. The House of Orange-Nassau has played a central role in the political life of the Netherlands. King's Day is celebrated on 27 April the birthday of the present king, Willem-Alexander. The entire country turns orange and repeatedly chants, *'Oranje boven, oranje boven. leve the Koning!* Orange on top, Orange on top. Long Live the King!' I always wore something orange on the day, regardless that the colour has never suited me.

16

Shipbuilder Peter the Great

When living in The Hague, I learned that Tsar Peter the Great of Russia went to the city incognito in 1697 to meet ordinary people. At two metres tall – in those days, the average Dutchman was about 1.65 metres – he was quickly found out. He received his royal welcome when he returned openly in 1717 and studied shipbuilding in Amsterdam for four months.

In a biography of the young tsar, Pulitzer Prize-winning author Robert Massie wrote that Peter could not understand why his own people produced only enough to feed themselves, yet more convertible wealth had been accumulated in Amsterdam than in all of Russia. Massie explains how Peter first learned about shipbuilding as a boy by constructing tiny ships on a Russian lake with Dutch friends. It led him on a European journey which included learning about the industry in Amsterdam and Deptford, the first of the Royal dockyards in England.

In Amsterdam, he worked as a ship's carpenter for the Dutch East India Company, later using his shipbuilding knowledge to strengthen the Russian navy. He was most famous for modernising Russia and making it into a major maritime power. But his dark side was also revealed to me at an exhibition at Amsterdam's Hermitage museum. His cruel executions, high taxes, violent tendencies, several revolts during his reign and his incomprehensible measures like the beard tax on bearded men. He had his eldest son Alexei tortured, leading to death from his wounds, for allegedly plotting the death of his father.

The Tsar Peter House in the shipbuilding district of Zaandam, eighteen kilometres from Amsterdam, is a humble dwelling where he stayed during his first eight days in the Netherlands in the seventeenth century. Fittingly, the old wooden house in which he slept was constructed from repurposed ship materials.

17

Drugs and prostitution

On a trip to Amsterdam as a teenager, I unknowingly bought a hash cake in a coffee shop and then wondered why I felt unusually relaxed after eating it. Now I take for granted the sweet, sickly smell of cannabis on the streets. But many visitors don't realise they can be fined and even sent to prison if in possession of up to five grams of the drug near schools or on public transport.

The Dutch law is complicated. For instance, cannabis can be sold over the counter in licensed coffee shops, which can store up to 500 grams at a time, but it is illegal to produce and supply the drug. This loose policy has led to an accelerating black market which the government has said it was planning to combat in 2021. The four-year experiment would start by targeting cafés in ten cities. Cannabis would be cultivated by nationally approved growers so the coffee shops in these locations could not deal with illegal growers. Cities where the drug's cultivation remains unregulated would be monitored and the results compared.

On its website, 4 November 2021, the government of the Netherlands said the first seven cannabis-growing farms for experiment were being established. The growers would legally produce hemp and hashish for sale in coffee shops in ten participating municipalities. The time that the farms and the municipalities needed for both would determine when the growers could start to supply coffee shops.

Revenue from coffee shops selling drugs and from red-light prostitution districts contribute slightly more than the Dutch consumption of cheese to the Netherlands gross domestic product.

Prostitution has been legal in the Netherlands since 2000. The Dutch government had hoped that by legalising it they would create an industry where independent sex workers could earn money unhindered by pimps. It didn't work out that way, according to Renate van der Zee, a Dutch writer with a focus on prostitution and human trafficking who has written several books on the Dutch sex industry. She claims that the Netherlands has not only failed to improve conditions for women in prostitution, but helped to create a market where international networks of human traffickers have exploited vulnerable women from poor countries, bought by men who justified their actions as legal.

In 2013, Amsterdam raised the minimum age for prostitutes from eighteen to twenty-one, but the city's oldest sex workers Louise and Martine Fokkens, seventy-two when I met them in 2015, were more concerned with the maximum age. I was part of a group who listened to their stories – published in several languages in their book *The Ladies of Amsterdam* – watched a video of their work and was invited to ask questions. When I brought up human trafficking, they denied any knowledge of it in their fifty-plus years in the profession. Someone asked if they had ever been in love. 'Of course, many times,' came the matter-of-fact answer as though it was a silly question. Martine had a regular and did not want to give him up.

A review in *The New York Times* of a documentary on the sisters called *Meet the Fokkens* gave a taste of their characters.

> When Martine Fokkens bustles into the small grocery store early in *Meet the Fokkens* she calls out a cheery hello to the man behind the counter. She has a purple hat and orange scarf framing her plump white face and a chihuahua tucked under an arm. What she needs, she announces, is a box of condoms. She was 69 when the movie was shot and enthusiastically plying her trade. Two years earlier her sister, Louise, had hung up her own riding crop because she said she 'couldn't get one leg over the other'.

The film portrayed Louise and Martine as coming from a fraught background of poverty, male violence and a fight for independence. But they did not explain, on screen or at our meeting, why prostitution seemed their best alternative.

18

Friesland and Mata Hari

The exotic dancer turned wartime spy Mata Hari who in 1917, at forty-one, was shot by a French firing squad, was born in Leeuwaarden, capital of the province of Friesland, 150 kilometres north of Amsterdam. Her statue stands on a canal bridge outside the hat shop that her grandfather started and her father inherited. Historians still argue over whether she was indeed a double agent, or even a spy at all. I searched for answers at the city's Fries museum but left still unsure about her motives.

Born Margaretha Geertruida Zelle in 1876, she attended a teacher's college and in 1895 married Rudolph MacLeod, a captain in the Dutch colonial army. From 1897 to 1902, they lived in Java and Sumatra, later divorcing on return to Europe. She began to dance professionally in Paris, changing her name to Mata Hari, a Malay expression for the sun (literally, 'eye of the day'). Credited with inventing the first striptease act, her numerous public affairs, many with military men, aroused the suspicions of the intelligence services. In February 1917, a French judge and police officers barged into Suite 113 of the luxurious Hotel Lycée on the Champs Elysées to arrest her. One account reported that she appeared naked and handed around chocolates in a captured German helmet.

The facts about her espionage activities are obscure. One story claimed that while she was living in The Hague in 1916, a German consul offered to pay her for whatever information she could obtain on her next trip to France. After her arrest by the French, she said only that she had given some outdated information to a German intelligence officer. According to statements that Mata Hari supposedly made, she had agreed to act as a French spy in German-occupied Belgium and did not bother to tell French intelligence of her prior arrangement with the Germans. The German government publicly exculpated her in 1930. The French dossier documenting her activities reportedly also declared her innocence.

The French historian Leon Schirmann alleged that the French government – desperate for triumphs and scapegoats at one of the most miserable periods of the war – seized on the opportunity to turn her into a wicked master-spy. She was the perfect victim, Schirmann argued, because she was foreign, manifestly immoral (by the hypocritical standards of the time) and a woman who lived the high life while French soldiers were dying. She has been labelled a cunning navigator of the patriarchy and a devious and manipulative femme fatale. I prefer assertions that she was bold and unapologetic – characteristics to be coveted as long as powerful, independent women are treated with hostility, no matter what century or country they live in.

After the museum, I strolled the streets of the old town trying to detect the Frisian language. Some 300,000 of Friesland's residents speak both Dutch and Frisian – the latter a Germanic language similar to both Dutch and English. I had run out of time to see Friesland's unique mudflats, laced into the Waddenzee (Wadden Sea), which are on UNESCO's World Treasures list. The slender islands across that body of water are rich with forests, dunes and beaches crossed by cycling paths, while the province's sixteenth-century fishing villages and port towns such as Hindeloopen and Harlingen are said to exude a relaxing charm.

19

Thinking of moving on?

One weekend, I jumped on a train to Voorberg, a pretty town not far from The Hague, for an open day of alternative medicine which included complimentary aromatherapy. Looking forward to a massage, I was instead diverted to a topic not on the agenda which interested me far more. As I was the first visitor, my host, I'll call her Marie, had time to chat. She once had a lucrative career in the frantic financial world of New York, with a comfortable home and busy social life. But she had long wanted to run a business focusing on her interests, find an intimate partner and travel. She had limited belief that she could achieve these three goals all together. Until she consulted Leslie, an astrocartographer in the US.

I had dabbled in astrology and done a course on developing psychic ability, both of which scuttled some of my suspicion of other-worldly matters, but this was a new term for me. Astrocartography is the study of planetary influences and how they can affect your geographic location. So if you are having sleepless nights figuring out if or where you should move for heightened well-being and the best opportunities, go to an astrocartographer.

Leslie drew up charts for Marie based on her date and time of birth. One key location was the Netherlands, where Marie eventually headed. Within two years, she had her own business, a partner and no regrets about changing her life so dramatically. Toying with moving on too, I also contacted Leslie. As her art and teaching career is her priority, she only takes on clients by word of mouth and prefers not to publicise her full name. She has been doing astrology, astrocartography and natal chart readings for forty years. She became interested after another guest at a health farm where she stayed compiled her charts, and she was stunned by the results.

My charts showed preferable locations were in the US on a line running from Chicago through to the southern states, including Louisiana, and on to Guatemala. The UK also was probable, but I had no interest in returning there. I did not pursue these possibilities at the time, but passed on Leslie's details to Catherine, a French friend who was considering moving to Canada or Asia. The charts Leslie sent Catherine pinpointed a north-south line halfway between Calgary and Vancouver as a potentially ideal home.

My friend ended up in Castlegar between Calgary and Vancouver, took a course at a college there, and only realised afterwards that it was on that exact line Leslie had mentioned. Although Catherine loved it there, she was unable to stay because of visa issues. She accepted a job offer in China but later returned to Alberta, where she said she never quite felt at home. Unforeseen circumstances later brought her back to Castlegar, where she says she is super-happy. She is even living in the same apartment as before. It came up for rent the exact month she needed to return.

20

New Orleans, April 2015

In a lull between work contracts, I decided to test my chart forecasts and went to New Orleans for twelve days. I had booked an Airbnb and planned my visit to coincide with the French Quarter and Easter festivals. My host Laurie's home was aptly named the Treehouse. She had it raised a further five metres (seventeen feet) so the top floor was above the trees after hurricane Katrina wrought huge destruction to the city in August 2005.

Even ten years after the storm, I found its emotional impact was still palpable in deserted outer areas where thousands of people once lived but became displaced persons. According to an Amnesty International report in 2015, the recovery process was plagued by the demolition of public housing and lack of adequate funds to help homeowners to rebuild. Gulf Coast residents simply could not afford to return.

'Think how it might make you feel different,' Leslie had said when I told her where I was going.

If that rather mysterious suggestion was connected to any sense of belonging or even homecoming I might experience, it did not happen during my visit. I was staying in a fairly isolated area with limited transport and no supermarkets nearby. My host had warned against going to some areas due to high crime rates but it didn't take me long to find the best way to walk to the historic Saint Charles Avenue streetcar. This streetcar line, which began operating in 1835, is claimed to be the oldest continuously operating one in the world.

In rambles along my neighbourhood's broad streets to catch the streetcar to the centre, I was entranced by spring-blossomed trees I later identified as dogwoods, natives of eastern North America and northern Mexico. Pink, white and reddish blossoms embellishing the creams, soft browns and yellows of elegant mansions, reminiscent of Tara, the palatial plantation home featured in the book and movie *Gone with the Wind*. The dogwood flowers are not actually flowers but bracts, which are modified leaves found in between a traditional leaf and the actual flower. The trees are most recognised for their cross-shaped white or pink bracts. Up close, you can see the dogwood's true flowers, which look like greenish-yellow clusters in the centre.

The mansions built in antebellum architecture combining Greek revival, Georgian and neoclassical styles typical of the Deep South, were usually plantation homes constructed before the American Civil War of 1861–1865. They reflected the power and idealism of wealthy landowners. But as antebellum is so interwoven with the memory of American enslavement, many people believe these buildings are not worth preserving or should be destroyed. One family of Creole women ran Laura Plantation for over sixty years, using slave labour. French, Creole, African, and American family members all played a part in the history told by the last Creole plantation owner, Laura Locoul Gore, in her 1936 memoir, *Memories of the Old Plantation Home*. Starting with Nanette Prud'Homme in 1808, they managed the business until 1891.

Laura was born on the family plantation in 1861. She died in 1963 at the age of 101, but her handwritten manuscript wasn't discovered until thirty years laer. On a tour to Laura Plantation, I was specially interested in the homes of slaves. One family lived in a cramped, wooden building with two or three separate rooms, including a kitchen, all sparsely furnished. Some slaves became entwined with the daily lives of their enslavers. Like Lucy Moore Jones, who accompanied her owners when they moved to Paris. A photograph of Lucy hangs on the wall in the museum space at the plantation. Others spent their lives in the sugar cane fields and were branded like cattle to keep them from running away.

21

Cajun and Creole

I attended a service at an Episcopal church on Easter Sunday. An informal, mostly doctrine-free event followed by a noisy Easter egg hunt and potluck lunch. The food was a mixture of Cajun and Creole. You see the terms everywhere in this vital, uninhibited city and throughout South Louisiana, on menus in particular, but you also hear them in discussions on architecture, history and music.

The Cajun people are descendants of French-Canadian settlers who first lived in Nova Scotia in 1605, an area they called l'Acadie. They were expelled when Canada fell to British rule, but regrouped when invited in 1764 to settle in the then Spanish colony of Louisiana. They incorporated cultural influences from their new Native American neighbours, and fellow settlers of German, Irish, Spanish, French and English descent, as well as African-descended people, both enslaved and free. The term Acadian morphed in English into Cajun. It was used largely as a derogatory term until it was reclaimed during Cajun pride movements in the mid-twentieth century.

Creole refers to people of European descent who were born in the French and Spanish colonies, but later often implied those of mixed European, African and occasionally Native American descent. You hear references to 'white Creoles' or 'old line Creole families', direct descendants of original French settlers to the city. Creole food is usually the traditional gourmet fare of this wealthy community, its multiple cuisine influences generally developed in the kitchens of enslaved women.

I spent many hours at the four-day French Quarter festival enjoying zydeco, a music genre that evolved in south-west Louisiana with French

Creole lyrics. It blends blues, rhythm and blues, and music indigenous to the Louisiana Creoles and the native American people of Louisiana. The festival is free, with some 2,000 artists to watch while strolling, sitting and maybe sipping a sazerac, one of the city's signature drinks. Created by New Orleans apothecary Antoine Amedie Peychaud in the 1830s, it is an intoxicating mixture of absinthe, whiskey and bitters, with a teaspoon of sugar.

22

Horn-tootin' steamboat captains

I could not leave New Orleans without a ride on the city's only paddle steamer, the *Natchez*. The Mississippi pilots were a special breed, each gifted with a phenomenal memory. To know the long, winding river at all was a considerable achievement, but to keep track of its constantly shifting sandbanks and shoals called for an art that was instinctive. The American writer Mark Twain, in his book *Life on the Mississippi*, describes how pilots would daily sit chatting on the bridge, apparently paying no attention to the calls of the man taking the depth of the water. Yet each call and any change in the position of a sandbank since the previous trip was instantly memorised.

Of the captains, four were formidable women. Captain Callie Leach French was a captain and pilot of the *New Sensation*; Mary Miller of the *Saline*; Mary Becker Green of the *Greene Line* – the only female steamboat captain in Ohio; and Blanche Douglass Leathers of the *Natchez VIII*.

Captain Mary Miller. who claimed to be the first, earned her licence on 18 February 1884.

Captain Callie Leach French, or 'Aunt Callie', as she was known, was described by her examiner as a 'bell-ringing, horn-tootin', wheel-turnin' captain'. On the river, she was captain and pilot from 1888 to 1907, but she also cooked, mended, nursed, acted, wrote jokes, never lost a boat or had an accident. Through it all, her strongest words were reported to be 'Well, I'll be dawg-goned!'

Mary Becker Greene became a pilot in 1896 and a captain a year later. She piloted the *Bedford* between Cincinnati and Louisville during

1897, but her biggest thrill was taking the *Greenland* steamer to the St Louis World's Fair in 1904, where the crowds reportedly went wild over her.

In 1891, Bowling Leathers and his wife Blanche built the *Natchez No. VIII*, which joined a fleet of seven. Blanche became a captain three years later.

23

Melbourne, October 2015–June 2017

I like to do something different whenever I return to Australia. This time, it was living in Victoria's capital of Melbourne. I had been there often over the years for work and leisure, enjoying its cultural, historical and culinary delights, though I had not experienced the worst of its unpredictable climate. When I began looking for work, friends, ten, fifteen years younger than me, warned that ageism was entrenched in the workplace. They were convinced they had been unsuccessful numerous times for that reason, despite the federal government's 2004 Age Discrimination Act. I assumed it would be difficult to prove this bias against the usual – albeit dubious – employer reasons for rejection, such as being overqualified, highly competitive, not quite the right fit and the like.

I found an abundance of online tips on how to prepare for a job where age might be a concern. One I noted was to downplay age by being forward-thinking. For example, having a firm grasp of new technologies, social media and an online portfolio – all of which I had. When these qualities were highlighted, an employer was more likely to look less at age and more at the candidate's drive to evolve.

When Myspace was launched in 2003, it fast became the largest social networking site in the world, reaching more than 100 million users per month. Rather than being a threat to the traditional journalism of my career, I saw the rapid growth of social media giants such as Facebook and Twitter as an opportunity to upgrade my knowledge. Perhaps the biggest effect of social media on traditional media and content is that now everyone feels like they have a voice, although its earlier growing influence was often dismissed.

Well-primed, I applied for hundreds of jobs with very few interviews. My resumé listed no more than twenty years' experience relevant to the position. At recruitment agencies, I was often given the impression that I needed to apologise for my lengthy overseas experience, which I had apparently wrongly assumed might have counted for something in Australia – a belief borne out by other unsuccessful recruits who had worked abroad. Disheartened, I finally went freelance. Ironically, the theme of one of my first assignments for a national weekly newspaper was age discrimination in the workplace. I had initially pitched them about a story on case studies of people who were losing the battle to survive on pensions below the poverty line.

My journalism had been focusing more on my specific global concerns, such as discrimination of all kinds. But my research for this article convinced me that of all discriminatory practices, ageism is the most socially normalised of any prejudice, and is not widely countered. I was shocked at the social issues it revealed. I have lived in enough countries of different cultures to know that ageism is rife. It can affect younger people as well as older ones of course, but the latter appears more widely spread. For example, in The Hague, having been offered a senior management position, the female human resources director I saw on my first day asked me how I had managed to finish a master's degree 'at my age'. Determined to not be defensive, I replied midly that education was for all ages. However, I couldn't resist adding that I had earned an academic excellence award. Lecturers told me how satisfying it was to have a student with many different perspectives on topics through life and careers experiences. A fellow student and I started Group 100 at the university for mature age students from twenty-one to 100+years.

The article was published in *The Saturday Paper* on 22 October 2016 as 'Interest on maturity'. It was also a finalist in the Older People Speak Out (OPSO) media awards in 2017. OPSO is a national all-volunteer group of retired and semi-retired professionals who collaborate with the media to be a voice and support for seniors. It was the brainchild of the late Val French, a journalist passionate about the fight for the rights of older people, the equality of women and the construction of a just and ethical society.

24

Interest on maturity

Linda, a former nurse from Queensland, is angry. 'It irks me greatly that if I am not a self-funded retiree, I am constantly being accused of being a burden on society,' she tells me. 'Politicians are blaming us instead of creating attitudinal change. Like giving the message to employers that older workers are valuable.'

While 1.5 million older Australians struggle to survive on an age pension barely above the poverty line of AU$426 a week, widespread age discrimination is forcing people out of the workforce. These people then face years on a Newstart allowance that has not increased in real terms since 1994. Over a quarter of older job seekers from the age of fifty have reported being affected by age discrimination.

Linda, now seventy-one, raised her three grandchildren after being granted full custody in 2002 because of abuse at the children's interstate home. She retired four years ago and works voluntarily on suicide prevention programs. Her seventeen-year-old grandson lives with her. Linda's pension is AU$877 a fortnight with some family tax benefit that will end in 2017. 'I am trying to meet my basic needs on the pension and those of my grandson,' she says. 'An extra AU$250 a fortnight would buy health and car insurance, internet, home and garden maintenance, haircuts, a dentist.' The retired nurse wants employers to be encouraged to keep people in the workforce for longer, and suggests that workplace 'quota systems' be introduced.

According to research economist Warwick Smith at Per Capita, one of the authors of the recent report *The Adequacy of the Aged Pension in Australia*, 'over a quarter of older job seekers from the age of fifty have reported being affected by age discrimination.' He says, 'When you combine this with the push to lift the pension access age to seventy, the rise of contract and casual employment, and the current and projected impact of technology on the demand for skills, the situation for many older workers looks grim.' The Chief Executive Officer (CEO) of the Australian Council of Social Service, Dr Cassandra Goldie, says the AU$38.38-a-day Newstart base rate was falling further behind the pension and community living standards because it is indexed to prices only, unlike pensions, which are indexed to wages.

The Adequacy of the Aged Pension in Australia, produced by the Benevolent Society and the Longevity Innovation Hub, as well as Per Capita, cites some pensioners taking drastic measures to make ends meet. They are turning off hot water in summer, blending food because they can't afford a dentist, and choosing whether to buy food or get essential medical prescriptions filled.

Cambodian-born Keo came to Melbourne as a refugee and single parent in 1987. She suffers from diabetes and other health issues, receiving a disability support pension of AU$794.80 a fortnight. 'If it wasn't for my daughter helping, I would have to choose between food and medication,' she says.

With Australia's pension spending at 3.5 per cent of gross domestic product – less than half the OECD average of 7.9 per cent – and its adequacy second-worst, those paying for rental accommodation are particularly hard hit, National Seniors Australia chief executive Dagmar Parsons advocates a review of the Commonwealth Rent Assistance appropriately indexed to private rental markets and a national expansion of affordable housing.

The aged pension report recommends establishing an independent age pension tribunal to determine a just base rate for the pension, similar in structure to the Parliamentary Remuneration Tribunal or the Fair Work Commission expert panel. The national Fair Go for Pensioners Coalition (FGFP) has for the past three years been urging the federal government for an urgent review of the retirement income system commissioned by the minister for social services – with no response. FGFP vice-president

Lew Wheeler says the review would cover all aspects of superannuation, Newstart allowance, the national partnership agreement on pensioner concessions and barriers to mature-age workforce participation.

It makes no economic sense not to employ older workers. As a recent report by the professional services firm PwC pointed out, an older workforce could deliver gains of up to AU$78 billion for the Australian economy. The Australian Human Rights Commission's Willing to Work national inquiry in May 2016 made fifty-six recommendations to combat employment discrimination against older people. Six years later, the report has had few if any outcomes.

While the report awaits action, people such as Julia, fifty-five, deal with harsh periods of homelessness and unemployment. The South Australian lost a highly skilled technical job, and has experienced severe homelessness. Julia gained a university degree in her forties in physics and chemistry, studying for ten years while a single parent. Unable to find a suitable job, she works in factories, does occasional private tutoring and cleaning. 'I was on the waiting list with the dental hospital for over a year and in quite a lot of pain. I blended food, lived on soup and lost a lot of weight,' she says.

Pas Forgione of Anti-Poverty Network, South Australia, says people like Julia are not to blame for a fundamental lack of jobs. 'Ironically it is at these times when the economy falters that the drive to attack and punish unemployed people and label them as dole bludgers intensifies,' he says.

Two organisations are helping unemployed older workers. Melbourne-based Marilyn and Howard King established Willing Older Workers in 2011 when Howard was unable to find work and Marilyn was studying mature-aged unemployment in Australia. It offers practical and emotional support. The other is olderworkers.com.au, a privately owned Australia-wide job board for over forty-fives. General manager Judy Higgins said many employers believed the commonly circulated myths about mature-age workers, such as: they are 'too slow, take more sick days, are no good with IT, are not willing to learn. None of this is true, but the age discrimination legislation is a blunt instrument that jobseekers find way too hard to use.'

Marilyn King is convinced the biggest drain on anyone relying on the pension is paying rent, even with some rental assistance.

If not for organisations such as Melbourne-based Housing for the Aged Action Group (HAAG) and its Home at Last Program, and the non-profit company Wintringham, which provides services to homeless older people in Victoria, many more people would be living on the streets. HAAG's latest report, *At the Crossroads in Retirement – Older People at Risk of Homelessness*, shows that nationally there has been a forty-four per cent increase in older people in insecure private rental housing over five years. Older people are spending on average sixty-five per cent of their pension in rent.

HAAG co-manager Fiona York says, 'There is a housing crisis but governments don't see it. We urgently need to invest in public housing for people over fifty-five. Many of the homeless are women aged seventy and above. They don't have any superannuation, have outlived their spouses, or had a family breakdown. The loss of two incomes to make rental payments is often the catalyst for homelessness and seeking housing assistance.'

The acting CEO of Wintringham, Michael Deschepper, says the more than 30,000 people registered on the Victorian Office of Housing list is evidence of the dire need not only for more supported affordable housing options but a concerted look at measures that could help prevent rent arrears, and other factors contributing to homelessness that could be avoided.

With the World Health Organisation forecasting nearly two billion people worldwide aged above sixty by 2050, the United Nations has urged its member nations to fight ageism – without addressing its own ageist practices.

In 2012, I applied for a communications role with UNESCO. I was told I was ineligible because the UN had a cut-off age for job applicants of fifty-seven and a compulsory retirement age of sixty-two.

Employees have to work a minimum of five years to qualify for its pension. Although my case was taken up by the Australian Human Rights Commission, it did not progress. The International Civil Service Commission has now recommended the retirement age be increased to sixty-five. But the UN policy flies in the face of the human right that everyone should be able to decide when or if they want to stop working – regardless of age.

As John from New South Wales puts it, 'I lost my job at sixty-five. I am seventy-one now and I want to work. I am technically savvy, my ability is ageless. All the stereotyping about older people's abilities or lack of them has no statistical foundation. But I am now locked into the system.'

A study, Generation Expendable, was started in mid-2020 when Australia's Covid pandemic fallout was first described as a 'shecession'. The report. published in October 2021 by Myfan Jordan, founding director of Melbourne-based Grassroots Research Studio, said in its conclusion,

> For the lucky few, the pandeconomy has provided new opportunities. For others, the rise of a mass exodus from the workplace, a 'great resignation' shows that workplaces the world over are no longer delivering for workers. For older women, already vulnerable to gendered ageing, the coronavirus crisis has amplified existing inequalities, including age and gender discrimination. Only by challenging entrenched hierarchies at work and in the home, will we be able to pivot to ways of working that support the wellbeing of all the community. To drive wellbeing at work for women, we need to rethink the workplace. Transformational policies such as a basic care income, cooperative ownership of the caring industries – commodified at work yet unvalued in the home – will support the dismantling of consumer capitalism and drive much needed change in the ways Australia works.

Following are three articles I published around that time on my other global concerns: asylum seekers, refugees and the environment.

25

Asylum seekers squat in empty buildings

I used to walk past what looked like a municipal building on my way to work at Greenpeace International in Amsterdam. The only signs of life were some people occasionally out on the front steps smoking. I asked around. What was it used for? Was it empty? I heard rumours that refugees were squatting there. Once my work contract ended, I went to investigate. A group of asylum seekers who had formed an organisation called We Are Here to draw attention to their tragic plight were squatting in the empty spaces, waiting, in vain it seemed, to be given refugee status. They were some of the thousands of asylum seekers squatting in empty buildings across the Netherlands. This is their story. It was published in *The New Internationalist* on 30 October 2015.

While the Netherlands is expected to take a further 7,000 refugees under the European Union's proposed quota plan, on top of the 2,000 already agreed to by the Dutch government in May, a stark question remains: what will happen to the numerous rejected asylum seekers – often waiting years and too scared to return to the countries they have fled – who are squatting in empty buildings across the country?

Although the Netherlands has agreed with the quota plan, unlike some eastern European countries and Baltic states, it would like to see better facilities in safe countries in the region, as there is no point in asylum seekers coming to a European country which refuses refuge, a spokeswoman for the Dutch Ministry of Security and Justice explained.

A contentious remark for We Are Here, an organisation of refugees which united in Amsterdam to promote their collective struggle. Its website proclaims the shameful way refugees are treated in the Netherlands. The organisation has some 225 immigrants from approximately fifteen countries. While their search for asylum has failed for now, they continue to appeal through various courts, including the Court of Justice of the European Union. They regularly demonstrate in Amsterdam's tourist-packed centres for what they want – a more generous refugee policy – while running the risk of being sent back to their country of origin or to the country of arrival in Europe. They want decent shelter. There is 'enough for everyone' they say.

One of the collective's coordinators, Luul – not her real name – has been squatting for a year with seventy-four other asylum seekers in an empty Amsterdam building owned by the Dutch municipality. She believes there are thousands of asylum seekers in the Netherlands who are waiting and hoping to, eventually, receive status.

Four hundred people are living on Amsterdam's streets, she says. Most of the time it's hard to live in squats. Evictions are regular. Churches and charities help, some live with friends. Although squatting is illegal in the Netherlands, squatters in Amsterdam are not evicted until the owner of the building has filed a report and proved they have serious plans for their property.

Luul was sixteen when, in 2010, she escaped from southern Somalia after being forced from her home by the Islamic militant group Al-Shabaab, which is allied to Al-Qaeda. The group recruited large numbers of children from school and abducted girls for forced marriage to fighters. Al-Shabaab demanded that Luul's fifteen-year-old brother become a soldier. 'My father said that his son would have no part of it. Two months later, my father was shot in a small mosque early in the morning,' she said. Her brother had died in a bomb explosion at his school.

'They took me to a man I was supposed to marry. I spat at him, insulted him, and was put in prison. A two-metre by one-metre prison cubicle. I was there for three weeks with three other girls. They refused us water. On some days we had food, on others none. They whipped us daily. For a long time, I thought I was going to die.

'Then another group came and there was a fight. Al-Shabaab ran, left us in the cells in the middle of the night. We started running, me and the other girls. I went to an aunt, who contacted my mother, and then my father's best friend, I called him uncle. He said he would get us out of the country as soon as possible. We had to leave or face being stoned to death.

'We started our journey by car. For almost a week, passing through controlled routes in Somalia and other countries. We were stopped once but the border guards did not know that Al-Shabaab was looking for us. Two of the girls with me were taken from the car, because they were not wearing burkas. It was too hot.'

These two teenage girls were later publicly shot by firing squad in the centre of the town of Beledweyne, near the border with Ethiopia. Al-Shabaab accused them of being spies for the Somali government.

Luul hid on her day's journey into Kenya in a net strung between the wheels of a mule cart. She made it with false documents to Europe. She was bound initially for Sweden but ended up transiting through Amsterdam, where she was sent to an adult detention centre.

'I was too tired to understand anything. I was treated like a criminal. I just wanted to feel safe again. To be told, don't worry, we are going to protect you. I was not supposed to be there for three weeks, but to go to an underage facility. To be rested. Become familiar with the new country.' Five years later, after learning Dutch at school, she continues to appeal to higher courts for refugee status.

She believes the immigration system does not work in a humane way. 'Asylum seekers are unprotected. There is no perspective on what they have suffered. They claim their stories are often not believed but how do they get proof? New proof of their stories is either impossible to get or would endanger their lives. They want to study, to work. But we are out on the street. We didn't expect to find ourselves in this situation when we came here as refugees. In fact, we lack all basic human rights. Where do we stay? First we stayed in a tent camp, followed by many different squatted buildings. What we need is a permanent solution.'

Asked why cases like Luul's are turned down, Yvonne Wiggers, spokesperson for the Dutch State Secretary of Immigration, Klaas Dijkhoff, said, 'It is not possible to say something about this particular case. But generally asylum seekers may be given asylum in the Netherlands if they need protection from persecution in their own country on account of their race, religion, nationality or beliefs. Or if they risk being tortured were they to return to their country.'

Ms Wiggers explained that it could take only eight days for asylum to be granted, this despite so many people waiting years for status. 'It could be longer, when, for example, immigration officials need to do more investigation. An asylum seeker does not need any evidence like photographs, but has to tell a credible story. They are checked, for instance if names and places don't add up in relation to the areas they said they had come from.'

Some members of We Are Here claim that they cannot return to their homelands. 'This may be true in some cases, but none of them has tried to get a *buiten schuld verklaring*, a document that confirms that it is not the refugee's fault that he or she cannot go back home and might make them eligible for legal status in the Netherlands.' Ms Wiggers said. Very few had requested the authorities help with finding documents of proof – a fact Luul denies. 'We asked, but did not get it.'

Ali Juma from Burundi has been waiting eleven years for refugee status. He says that he has been constantly turned down because there was not enough evidence to prove his claim of persecution. Now the Red Cross is involved and tracking down his family and friends for proof of his story. 'Red Cross has no power in First World countries. It has more impact to approach them for help in developing countries,' he said. This problem was not something that had occurred to him. Why wasn't he informed this was possible rather than waiting for more than a decade? He has no answer.

We are Here also claims the Dutch government is violating the Geneva Convention by denying the basic human right for protection and safety. Jasper Karman, spokesperson for Amsterdam's mayor, Eberhard van der Laan, said courts had ruled that the shelters known as 'Bed, Bath and Bread' (BBBs) made available by the municipality of Amsterdam meet the legal requirements for providing shelter at night. They are for refugees who have exhausted their asylum options.

Karman said that the BBB shelter opened every day at five p.m., providing dinner, a hot shower, a bed, room to store personal belongings in, a laundry room, and breakfast. When it closed at nine a.m. the residents were given two tram tickets to travel to a doctor, a location where activities were being organised or the city centre. The supervised buildings were usually old schools or empty children's day care centres.

'We have deliberately made the decision not to offer twenty-four-hour shelter as most of the refugees request, because then we would be offering the kind of shelter that is the ministry's domain. This would not only be illegal, but would undermine our constructive relationship with The Hague, and we need to find a solution for this difficult problem,' Karman said. 'We have made it very clear that under no circumstances will we create more than these 135 shelter places. Amsterdam cannot solve this problem alone and cannot by itself offer refuge to a seemingly endless stream of refugees.'

A 2013 Amnesty International report on the detention of irregular migrants and asylum seekers echoes similar recommendations made in its first report in 2008. The Ministry of Security and Justice has drafted a new Return and Aliens Detention Bill which addresses some of the concerns. Under the new law, foreign nationals will have more freedom while being held in detention than they do now. For instance, they will be able to move freely within the detention centre between eight a.m. and ten p.m. with minimal supervision; be entitled to at least forty hours of daytime activity each week and be allowed to make phone calls on their mobile phone (but cannot use the phone's camera or have internet access).

The recommendations from Amnesty International's report include

- establishment of a rights based, all-inclusive approach to irregular migration in which measures to 'combat' irregular

migration and crimes such as human trafficking and other human rights violations and abuses are balanced with increased protection for the victims;
- immigration detention should be used only if, in each individual case, it is demonstrated that it is a necessary and proportionate measure in conformity with international law;
- provide traumatised asylum-seekers and victims of human rights violations with the necessary time and means to prepare their asylum applications;
- under no circumstances should victims of human trafficking be penalised for their illegal entry into the Netherlands or be administratively detained while awaiting their expulsion. Neither should victims of human trafficking be prosecuted for crimes committed where they have been compelled to do so.

Asked why the recommendations had not been addressed despite the first report coming out seven years before, Ruud Bosgraaf, senior press officer in Amnesty's Amsterdam office, explained that it was a sensitive issue in Dutch politics between both parties in the coalition government, the Labour party and the People's Party for Freedom and Democracy. 'The lawmaking process sometimes takes years and years in this country,' he said.

These kinds of explanations are not what displaced people seeking a permanent, safe home want to hear.

On returning to Amsterdam in 2019, I learned that most of those I had interviewed, including Luul, were still waiting for refugee status.

26

Former refugee boats cruise Amsterdam canals

Anas, a Syrian guide, tells tourists on a former refugee boat cruising Amsterdam's canals he has a simple solution to stop people smuggling. He says desperate people from countries where it's almost impossible to get a visa to hoped-for destinations would gladly pay embassies rather than people smugglers if governments would open the door to obtain visas. 'Specific arrangements and categories would be necessary according to people's needs but this would be an organised, legal way to save lives. Countries could use the money to help secure flights for refugees and arrange resettlement,' he said.

Anas (not his real name) told me he paid almost €5,000 ($7,463) for him and his wife to be taken by boat from Turkey to Greece with 128 other refugees. From there, they made their way to the Netherlands and were granted political asylum.

Lampedusa Cruises in Amsterdam is a collective of members from countries including Egypt, Eritrea, Syria, Somalia and the Sudan. The captains and guides are refugees who intertwine their often gruelling stories with the influence immigration has had on the city's history.

Teun Castelein, a Dutch artist and founder of the project, explains, 'Here we have a big tradition of pleasure-boating, but I couldn't watch it any more without thinking of migrants of the Mediterranean.'

Castelein visited the Italian island of Lampedusa, an entry point into Europe for thousands of refugees, and persuaded the mayors of Lampedusa and Amsterdam to help bring two refugee boats to the Netherlands. The art-social project about immigration began in 2016. Other team members include a Dutchwoman, Felice Plijter, who has

Former Egyptian refugee Hatim 'Tommy' Sherif describes the sights of Amsterdam to visitors, as well as his experiences as a refugee, on canal cruises in a former refugee boat.

been teaching bicycle mechanics to refugees. Lampedusa Cruises' two boats are the flagship *Alhadj Djumaa* (formerly *Meneer Vrijdag*), also known as *Mr Friday* and *Hedir* (powerful voice in Arabic), which was formerly called *Kleine Boot*.

As *Hedir* is steered through the canals by a Somalian named Yousef, often backing up to avoid busy water traffic on this balmy day, Anas shares his delight at the chance to study for a Master of Business Administration in The Hague. 'Now I can start to feel integrated,' he says with a smile.

Another guide on Lampedusa with an often harrowing story to tell is Egyptian refugee Hatim ('Tommy') Sherif. He is a storyteller on a schools circuit in the Netherlands. After the Arab Spring of 2011, he began working with the Muslim Brotherhood. He resisted pressure to become a politician, describing himself as a 'go-between'. In Cairo, in 2012, he worked for TV channels as a researcher and began helping Syrian refugees find jobs and houses, and gave them money. 'I thought one day I might be one,' he says.

Following the 2013 military coup, which overthrew then president Mohamed Morsi, Tommy was arrested and tortured on what he says were false charges. He was pressured to spy on the Muslim Brotherhood but refused. 'I had been preparing for torture by increasing my weight by sixteen kilograms to cushion me from beatings,' he said. He fled

*'Every time I step into the boat I feel like it's the first time and I feel at home,'
Tommy says of his work on the former refugee boats in Amsterdam.
(Photo Louisa van der Meij)*

Egypt shortly afterwards and sought asylum in the Netherlands. Now, with refugee status, he has written a book about his time in the detention centre at Amsterdam's Schiphol Airport. He says he is beginning to feel like he belongs.

In February 2022, Tommy told me he had made three documentaries in the past four years, including his first play as a director and actor. Working with Lampedusa Cruises had opened many doors for him, he said.

A wooden cross made from pieces of a boat wrecked off the coast of Lampedusa, Italy, on 11 October 2013, is displayed in the British Museum, London; 366 Eritrean and Somalian refugees were drowned on the boat en route from Libya to Europe. Lampedusa residents helped save the lives of 155 others. After meeting some of the Etritean Christian survivors in the church on Lampedusa, Francesco Tuccio, the island's carpenter, fashioned them each a cross from the wreckage of the boat as a reflection on their salvation and hope for the future.

A similar cross was made for Pope Francis, who carried it at a memorial service for those who had perished. Tuccio made the piece for the British Museum to mark an extraordinary moment in European history and the fate of Eritrean Christians.

Published in *The Australian*, 20 October 2017

27

On the sustainable honey highway

Sustainability champion Deborah Post's idea to establish one of the world's first honey highways in the Netherlands has global reach as insect populations decline and nine per cent of all bee species in Europe are threatened with extinction.

The International Union for Conservation of Nature has already warned that increased farming intensification has led to degradation of bee habitats. It says that vigorous silage production – at the expense of haymaking – causes losses of herb-rich grasslands and season-long flowering, important sources of forage for pollinators. Insecticides also harm wild bees and herbicides reduce the flowers they depend on.

The honey highway was one of seventeen Dutch innovations at the 2017 Ideas for Europeevent held at the Afsluitdijk in the Netherlands. Deborah told guests, including former UN Secretary General Kofi Annan, how the highway, a seven-kilometre stretch of the A4 between Delft and Schiedam, aims to save 350 species of wild bees and the original Dutch honey bee. The solution to saving bees was, she said, 'as old as the road to Rome – sowing wild flowers'.

Deborah is contracted to Rijkswaterstaat, ProRail and dyke wardens who allocate land for her work. She promotes their sustainability agenda by giving bags of honey highway seeds to neighbourhoods, sowing wild flowers with schoolchildren and placing biodynamic beehives on land near the highway. She also organises biodynamic bee courses. Biodynamics is an alternative form of farming which includes concepts based on the ideas of philosopher Rudolph Steiner's book *Bees*. Its forecast that insects would die out prompted Deborah's mission. She was also influenced by Professor Piet Zonderwijk's book *De bonte berm (The Variegated Verge)*, which espoused the idea that wild plant species grow in greater abundance when the berm is correctly managed.

Deborah acquired her first swarm after attending a biodynamic beekeeping course, but the insects began to die. 'I was sad because the trees and flowers were in bloom, but still the bees couldn't find enough food. I got another swarm and 100 organic apple trees from a friend.'

After a golf club gave her land for the trees, she let the bee colony swarm. Another colony arrived and the hives expanded. Determined to extend food supplies, she developed organic wild flower seed that contains forty-four types of flowers and herbs. Her idea to sow the roadsides of the A4 was enthusiastically encouraged and the honey highway opened in November 2015. Annual organic bee dinners, which Deborah holds at her family's country house in Schipluiden, between Rotterdam and The Hague, have convinced hundreds of people of her vision.

'There is clean soil and no pollution on 17,000 kilometres of dykes and 14,000 kilometres of railways and no pollution at roadsides,' she says. 'We have 20,000 kilometres of highways and in each of the eleven regions of the Netherlands there are about 500 kilometres of provincial ways. We always choose the right places for sowing.' On the annual national sowing day on 7 June, thousands of schoolchildren plant at roadsides, dykes, in their own gardens, and on grounds next to schools.

Deborah hopes alumni will ask their employers to help fund the projects or offer land. Autumn projects included sowing roadsides in a sustainable neighbourhood in Rijswijk, on land owned by an organic vegetable grower in Brielle, and a roadside in The Hague. Land is being prepared on highways in Friesland, as are dykes in South Holland and the South Holland islands.

Reflecting on her motivations, Deborah told me, 'I have an ideal, a purpose. I pushed away huge obstacles. I received encouragement because I believed in myself, and because what I am doing is good for

Mother Nature, people and society.' Deborah told me in February 2022 that Honey Highway is now a total national concept with 500 kilometres of blooming roadsides and company-sponsored business parks.

Published in Rotterdam School of Management *Outlook* magazine, 1 December 2017

28

Volunteering exploits experience

Prospective employers sometimes asked if I was interested in voluntary work, as though my qualifications and experience were not worth a wage. I temporarily swallowed my objections to working for no payment when I took on two jobs in Melbourne for strong personal reasons. One was as a radio journalist and presenter at 3CR community radio station where I co-hosted a program called *City Limits*. The other was a convenor of a neighbourhood program under a national street by street campaign.

The station, which was Melbourne's first community radio to obtain a licence in 1976, hosts 130 programs by more than 400 volunteers. It began digital broadcasting in 2010 and was part of the Commit to Community Radio campaign three years later, which convinced the federal government to extend funding for community radio digital broadcasting until 2016. Over thirty shows now publish a podcast on the website. I enjoyed 3CR as I had wanted to expand on my radio journalism while learning the technical aspects of running a show. The station, which included political and environmental themes, gave me free rein to initiate my own ideas. For instance, an International Women's Day program I presented on superannuation anomalies and gender pay gap issues affecting women created much support for action.

I also worked with a tireless woman called Irene Opper and other volunteers in a street by street project in our various neighbourhoods to create a better sense of community. The campaign's mission was part of a national program to combat isolation, to see connecting with neighbours become normal across Australia, and for people to feel happier, safer and more supported as a result. One social event I organised brought some people together who had lived in the same small street for forty years but never spoken. I had started to think that my early positive experiences of friendly communities when an immigrant in Brisbane were very different. Perhaps people are more wary of each other now, specially in cities with high crime rates.

I bought a studio apartment in St Kilda, not realising the popular beachside suburb was fast becoming a centre for the use of the drug referred to as 'ice'. It is a form of methamphetamine, an addictive stimulant that is sold and used illicitly. Once a week, I helped prepare an evening meal at a community kitchen run by the local Baptist church and got to know the regulars. One, a former doctor, had lost a lot of his coordination after a near fatal accident and could not work any more. Another was a well known actress, accompanied by her intellectually disabled adult son. She recounted amusing stories about her roles and experiences on popular Australian TV shows such as *Prisoner*. I missed them when they moved to another area she much preferred because it was drug-free.

29

Hungary and medical tourism, 2017

I turned to medical tourism in Hungary when diagnosed with posterior tibialis tendonopathy. The posterior tibialis tendon is one of the most important tendons in your leg. It attaches the posterior tibialis muscle on the back of your calf to the bones on the inside of your foot, supporting your foot and holding up its arch when walking. Melbourne specialists could not diagnose why it had happened but recommended urgent surgery. The hospital which served St Kilda said it was not an emergency. It promised to contact me about joining a long waiting list, but failed to do so. Other hospitals my GP had asked to help also refused to accept me. I continued to treat myself with expensive foot supports, and other aids like ineffective physiotherapy, until I could wait no longer.

Having worked in Hungary for several years, the country was my preferred choice for the surgery. Notably, of its thirteen Nobel prizes, three were for medicine. Its medical tourism association (MTA) linked me by email to an Hungarian orthopaedic surgeon. I checked his profile, sought references and made an appointment to see him in July at a private medical centre in Budapest. Next I arranged to stay in an Airbnb in Amsterdam for two months to allow time to explore other options, including having the surgery in the Netherlands.

I left Australia on 26 June 2017. Two MTA representatives met me at Budapest airport on my arrival in July for my medical appointment. Unbeknown to me at the time, one of them had vacated his apartment near the medical centre for my three-night stay, at a reasonable rate. I was impressed by the specialist, unlike my experience with the Netherlands medical system, where the doctor I saw a second time at a private clinic did not even recall my first visit or what exactly was wrong with me. A date for the surgery in Budapest was set for 27 September.

After the operation, I would be restricted to non-weight-bearing for six weeks. The first two weeks would be in a plaster of Paris splint. Then a cast for four weeks, followed by a special boot for another six weeks. Once this time was up, I had to wear an ankle brace for two months in the daytime but would be able to walk.

Before leaving the Netherlands for Hungary in September, I took my last holiday for some time. I went to Adlestrop in Gloucestershire, England.

30

Poet Edward Thomas and Adlestrop

I first heard about Adlestrop when on a tourist train in Castlemaine, Victoria, Australia, in March 2017. The train stopped a little longer than usual at a station but no one got off or on. My companion, a signals engineer and train buff, said it reminded him of a poem a poet had written when his train had stopped for a short time at Adlestrop in England not long before the outbreak of World War I.

My curiosity aroused, I discovered the poet was Edward Thomas and his poem was called 'Adlestrop'. On 24 June 1914, the train on which Thomas and his wife Helen were travelling from London to the Gloucestershire village of Dymock to visit Thomas's close friend and mentor, American poet Robert Frost, stopped briefly at Adlestrop. Four days later, Archduke Franz Ferdinand was assassinated in Sarajevo, set-

The only evidence that the English poet Edward Thomas was at Adlestrop's now closed railway station is a bench in the village bus shelter bearing a plaque with his poem 'Adlestrop' engraved on it.

Edward Thomas in 1912. (Photo: E.O. Hoppe/Corbis)

ting in motion a chain of events that would culminate in the declaration of the war in early August. The peace that most of Europe had enjoyed since 1815 was shattered.

For most of his adult life, Thomas lived by writing prose. He wrote topographical works, biographies, critical studies, one novel, some experimental prose pieces, and essays about nature. He had a focus on English countryside poems.

I visited Adlestrop with my train buff friend on 15 August. The station was closed; it operated between 1853 and 1966. The only evidence of the Thomas connection was a bench in the village bus shelter bearing a plaque with the poem engraved on it. Thomas's field notebooks showed that his train stop was made at twelve forty-five p.m., which corresponded to a scheduled down stopping service, not an unscheduled stop by an express as described in the poem.

Although not, strictly speaking, a war poem, Adlestrop became popular in anthologies because of its reference to a peaceful time and place only a short time before the outbreak of the war. Thomas enlisted in the British army in 1915 to fight and was killed in action during the Battle of Arras in 1917, soon after he arrived in France. It was just before the poem was to be printed in his collection *Poems*. It was published in the *New Statesman* three weeks after his death.

Adlestrop

Yes, I remember Adlestrop –
The name, because one afternoon
Of heat the express-train drew up there
Unwontedly. It was late June

The steam hissed. Someone cleared his throat.
No one left and no one came
On the bare platform. What I saw
Was Adlestrop – only the name

And willows, willow-herb, and grass,
And meadowsweet, and haycocks dry,
No whit less still and lonely fair
Than the high cloudlets in the sky.

And for that minute a blackbird sang
Close by, and round him, mistier,
Farther and farther, all the birds
of Oxfordshire and Gloucestershire.

Edward Thomas

After reading the poem, I needed convincing why it resonated so much with the public. The Matthew Hollis book *Now All Roads Lead to France: the Last Years of Edward Thomas* sheds light on the reasons. 'Sixteen lines, none of expressive rhythm so championed by Frost. None of his dramatic narrative. Perhaps something to do with the lazed, heat-filled atmosphere it evokes the last summer before the war. Its provenance six weeks before the start of the conflict. Its drafting less than six months later. Or the inscrutable chorus of birdsong into which the poem dissolves.' According to Hollis, it was not necessarily the pinpointing of any particular event or episode that stirred the poem to life, but something about the wordlessness of thought and memory. The power of recall. The notion that the senses are capable of remembrance; that the mind can overcome things lost or misplaced to travel across place or time.

Robert Frost's well-known poem *The Road Not Taken* opens with the line 'Two roads diverged in a yellow wood.' It referred to the frequent woodland walks he and Thomas enjoyed in Dymock. The poem was actually written for Thomas during a period of indecision. It was 1915. Frost had returned to the US, while Thomas was intending to follow him there. But as the war was still raging Thomas's conscience held him back. He did not want to enlist but, as he explained in a letter to his friend, 'hardly a day passes without my thinking I should'.

The Hollis biography of Thomas explained that Frost's poem had been understood by some as an emblem of individual choice and self-reliance. A moral tale in which the traveller takes responsibility for their own destiny. He goes on to argue that Frost never intended it to be read that way, although well aware of the playful ironies contained within it. Instead, it carried a more personal message to Thomas. But the English poet felt the poem was a rebuke rather than the teasing that was intended. He enlisted not long after reading it. Nevertheless, the two poets' friendship had been invaluable in unlocking Thomas's creativity. Without which perhaps he would never have turned from prose to poetry.

31

Budapest, September 2017

After finding an apartment to rent for my estimated time in Hungary, my next priority was to secure post-surgery help for at least twelve weeks. I asked a college where I had once given journalism lectures if they could advertise the paid work internally. As a result, six students worked for me by roster. I also employed a nurse for the first two weeks after leaving hospital. Their help became even more important when a week after my foot surgery I had a huge shock. I had breast cancer.

It had been detected after I developed an internal infection in hospital while recovering from the foot operation. I was sent to a gynaecologist, who also asked if I wanted a mammogram. I agreed, although it had been only eleven months since the last clear screening in Melbourne. Events then escalated. The gynaecologist found a lump. A radiologist gave me a deep, painful biopsy which brought tears, and told me I had a malignant tumour in my left breast. How could he know without final results? But he was right. How could this happen? As I had been taking hormone replacement therapy (HRT) for many years, I had been rigorous about annual mammograms and biopsies. I had been reassured about an inverted nipple at several of my screenings and had not felt this lump.

Before deciding what to do, I sought recommended oncologist opinions in several countries, spoke to friends who had recovered from the disease and even tried hemp, which had been reported as sometimes helping to shrink tumours. I took a few drops a day for almost three weeks and then had another mammogram at a different clinic. In that time, I felt that I had taken back control of how I could manage the condition, and it just might work. According to Hungarian law, it is legal to cultivate hemp if it contains less than 0.2% THC (tetrahydrocannabinol) – the psychoactive compound in cannabis that makes you high. The label on the hemp said it was THC-free. The second mammogram showed the tumour had actually grown slightly larger at 2.3 centimetres. I had surgery on15 December.

I refused any follow-up treatment, but decided to stop taking HRT. Not because I believed it caused cancer. Tests after the surgery had revealed that I was oestrogen and progesterone receptor-positive. For twenty-eight years, I had swallowed small daily doses of the hormones oestrogen and progesterone. Receptors are proteins in or on cells that can attach to certain substances in the blood. Normal breast cells and some breast cancer cells have receptors that can attach to these two hormones and depend on them in order to grow. Cancers are called hormone receptor-positive or hormone receptor-negative based on whether or not they have these receptors. As my tumour was oestrogen and progesterone receptor-positive, I did not want to pump more of the hormones into me.

Two male oncologists told me to stop taking HRT at once, which I refused, instead following the advice of a female oncologist to withdraw from it gradually over nine weeks. I bought various supplements from a naturopath which did not contain the two hormones in case I had the menopause I had never had. It was not as bad as I expected but for months there were negative mood changes. A flat almost numb feeling with no sense of well-being, and some hot flushes. Many times I was tempted to go back on it. It had improved my life so much.

32

The benefits of HRT

It was 1990 when my body started to warn me. I had just arrived for a posting at the Australian Embassy in Brussels, a demanding job running its public affairs and cultural programs, committed to making Australia's image count – a difficult task in a Europe immersed in the collapse of communism. I arrived in Belgium, determined that my work would not be affected by the injuries sustained in a head-on car crash in Canberra eight months before I was due to go overseas.

I had been a front-seat passenger in a utility vehicle when a driver on the opposite side of the road had, it seemed, deliberately turned her steering wheel and smashed into the vehicle my husband was driving. Police told me later they were convinced it was a suicide run. The driver had been fighting with her boyfriend and both had stopped taking medication for their medical conditions. The driver of the other car died after crashing into our vehicle and hitting another car behind.

I was in hospital for two months, including two weeks in intensive care, with many broken bones, and a collapsed lung. My body twisted in a different posture.

I remember being drip-fed Christmas dinner as nurses were returning laughing from their traditional lunches. I recovered in traction. Surgery was not recommended because of the punctured lung. My surgeon told me the left hip had been so badly injured that I could expect three hip replacements in a lifetime because of the risks of osteoporosis. (I had one eighteen years later in 2006 and hope that is the last.) I revised my French in the two months in hospital after the accident to prepare for my posting – the new job my incentive to recover as quickly as possible. But once at the embassy, it was another health issue that began to worry me more.

I began menstruating every one or two weeks. A doctor suspected the onset of premature menopause. It generally starts for women in their mid-forties, but also can begin in the late thirties and early forties. I was prescribed HRT. Two tablets a day of 0.625 milligrams of oestrogen, and five milligrams of progesterone. My periods stopped completely. My doctor said it was normal with this dosage and if I wanted to continue menstruating, then the tablets could be reduced. The familiar surged back with a vengeance when I tried that. I increased the dose and did not menstruate again or have menopause.

'Where do you get your energy?' had been a usual question when I was taking the hormones. I have maintained a sharp career focus, travelled the world, lived/worked in countries where climates were debilitating, and had much younger friends and romantic partners who complained about keeping up with me. HRT helped me greatly by balancing my hormones and mood swings. I declared many times to doctors that I would take HRT until my life ended and most agreed – if I was healthy with no side effects. In 2002, news broke of a link between HRT use and breast cancer. I was working for an aid agency in the Federated States of Micronesia at the time. My doctor in Australia told me to wait until I returned before deciding whether to stop it, as I could experience distressing withdrawal symptoms. By the time I returned, another report disputed the earlier one and I stayed on it. I stopped taking HRT a few years later after reading yet another risk report, but very unpleasant symptoms sent me quickly back on the pills. Until 2018.

33

The cycle ends, 2018

I have now lived and worked in ten different countries and, by my last count, visited fifty-six. There has always been a reason to move on, usually work-related, but once I resigned from a secure job in Australia to be closer to my mother in England as her health was failing. I had first taken leave, conditional on returning in several months or resigning. I arrived back in Hungary with an English as a second language teaching diploma, and began a contract at a high school. I lasted a few months teaching unruly fourteen- to sixteen-year-olds before deciding to leave. Not to give up on this fresh vocation, despite misgivings, but to try varied roles in different countries and expand my experience. I had only had the offer of six weeks at an international summer school in England when I left the school in May 2007. I wrote the resignation letter giving up my Australian job as a magazine editor and digital content manager. I waited a full day before I sent it, beset by fears of the insecurity ahead. But sure that this time my mother needed me most.

Despite my travels, I have seen a lot of my family over these cycles. My son Shaun, his partner Sarah and my two grandchildren, Ewan and Thea, live in Sydney. Ewan was almost three when his parents took him to Montenegro, where I was working in 2008. Now sixteen, he says he remembers eating painted hard-boiled eggs for the orthodox Easter event there. Ewan was nine when he and his dad returned to Europe to visit me in Amsterdam on New Year's Eve 2014, and relatives in the UK. Five years later, my granddaughter Thea, then also nine, arrived in Europe with her dad for the first time. We met in the Netherlands, where I had been spending Christmas, and then flew to Hungary for their remaining two weeks. With internet, I can virtually sit at their summer evening barbecues surrounded by palms while I eat breakfast watching snow falling, see gifts being unwrapped on special days, and know how well connected we are in every sense of the word.

The Hungarian language is less of an obstacle than when I first went to the country in 2003. One of the big surprises when I returned in 2017 was that all travel announcements on Budapest public transport were in English as well as Hungarian, capitalising on the tourist boom. The English woman behind the voice, Rachel Appleby, speaks Hungarian, although she agreed with me how tough it was to learn, sometimes doing a very quick revision of difficult-sounding place names before announcing them. She likened learning the language to the Rubik cube which was invented in 1974 by Hungarian sculptor and professor of architecture Ernő Rubik. Rachel has tried unsuccessfully to work out the moves and twists of the puzzle. There were also twists in Hungarian to be resolved before she could speak it better, its logic was so different from the logic of other languages she had learned, she told me. As well as the English travel announcements, English translations are on all major notices and billboards, on exhibits in museums and at concert halls and other institutions. Students can take subjects in English at most of Hungary's universities.

In my introduction, I spoke about my search for the inner assurance that Jung described as individuation. Many of the people in this book – historic and contemporary – have taken risks, dared to be different, and accepted the consequences. The most telling factor of their lives was the belief they had in themselves, ignoring their critics to follow their own often arduous paths. Some reached out across centuries. The inviolable connection of nature united Spinoza to Van Gogh and Cézanne. But I have yet to fully realise my quest.

Completely understanding myself can appear unreachable as behaviour, attitude and beliefs fluctuate, dictated to by specific responses to particular circumstances. I have long-ago secrets hidden in the darkest corners of my early life which are too confronting to face, let alone reveal. I have therefore come to the more enlightening conclusion that the ultimate aim of individuation is to create an enduring gift for the world. I am hopeful that is possible to achieve without all the conditions that Jung imposed.

34

Budapest, March 2022

It has taken a global pandemic to find the perfect example of a pioneer who has delivered such a gift. She is Hungarian Katalin Karikó, whose work is now the basis of the Covid-19 vaccines marketed by Pfizer/BioNTech and Moderna. I was filled with pride when I found out. A perplexing reaction that strengthened my tenuous belief that this country was becoming home.

The biochemist struggled for years to convince colleagues that messenger RNA could have disease-fighting applications in humans. It is a component of DNA, considered to be one of the main building blocks of life.

In 1985, Dr Karikó, her husband and two-year-old daughter moved from Hungary to Philadelphia, Pennsylvania, so she could take a postdoctoral position at Temple University. Her first mRNA-therapy grant application was rejected in 1990 a year after she joined the faculty at the University of Pennsylvania.

According to interviews she has given, Dr Karikó faced sexism early in her career. Once, she was asked for the name of her supervisor while running her own lab. She was referred to as 'Mrs' in an article in which her male colleagues were given the title 'Professor'. Then came more rejections, job losses, and continuing disbelief about her findings. But she never gave up.

In 2005, she found a way to configure mRNA so that it bypassed the body's natural defenses – a discovery that paved the way for the world's first mRNA vaccines. Now senior vice president at BioNTech RNA Pharmaceuticals in Germany, she has received many awards.

They include the Swiss Academy of Pharmaceutical Sciences prestigious Reichstein Medal and the Carnegie Foundation's Great Immigrants Award. She was also named one of *Time* magazine's 100 most influential people. In its edition 27 September– 4 October 2021, Nobel prize winning American biochemist Jennifer Doudna, in a tribute to Dr Karikó, wrote, 'Katalin inspires us with her creativity, persistence and commitment to defeating this pandemic and mitigating future health threats.'

Perhaps her most apt award was the Semmelweis prize, due to its link to the Covid-19 protective rule of regular hand washing. Hungarian obstetrician Ignaz Semmelweis discovered the disease-fighting power of hand washing in 1847. Semmelweis disproved the belief that post-operations deaths were caused by 'poison air' in a hospital ward. His work all but removed puerperal fever from the maternity units he worked in. His colleagues and superiors derided his work while he was alive but antiseptic surgery drastically reduced post-operation fatalities.

Brexit has come and gone. I am a legal resident with the same rights I had before as a UK national in an EU country. I have two different-shaped feet because the injured one was rebuilt. The balance is corrected with custom-made insoles which I have to use for life. Three years after a Melbourne hospital turned me down for urgent surgery, it asked if I would agree to a video conference about possible surgery for my tendonitis. My questioning of the long delay was explained, in part, by the general manager of surgical services: 'There are times when the hospital does not meet the expectations of patients and I am sincerely sorry this has been your experience.' I hate to think how my condition would have deteriorated in those three years had I stayed in Australia. As it was, the Hungarian surgeon had to break the bones at the back of the foot and reset them as they had bent so much.

I never suspected that my mother's forward-thinking when I was fifteen would drive me onto a path with so many diverse detours. Like many of the people in this book, my physical, mental, and intellectual energies rarely sap. Those elements need revelation to nourish them. Even a revolution of original ideas. A personal legacy that would finally earn that assurance I want.

Bibliography

Asmelash, Leah & Willingham, A.J. She was demoted, doubted and rejected. Now, her work is the basis of the Covid-19 vaccine. CNN. (17 December 2020) https://edition.cnn.com/2020/12/16/us/katalin-kariko-covid-19-vaccine-scientist-trnd/index.html

At Eternity's Gate (2018), Directed by Julian Schnabel (biographical drama). The film was theatrically released in the United States on 16 November 2018 by CBS Films.

Brkanic, Dzana. UN Court confirms Ratko Mladic's Life Sentence for Genocide. BIRN (8 June 2021). https://balkaninsight.com/2021/06/08/un-court-confirms-ratko-mladics-life-sentence-for-genocide/

Claretie, Jules. *L'Art Francais en 1872*. Japonisme, or Japonism, is a French term that was first used by Claretie in this book. It refers to the influence of Japanese art on Western art. Forgotten Books (reprint 23 April 2020). https://www.thegreatbritishbookshop.co.uk/collections/art/products/nouvelles-archives-de-lart-francais-1872-recueil-de-documents-inedits-publies-par-la-societe-de-lhistoire-de-lart-francais-classic-reprint

Conrad, Joseph. *Heart of Darkness*. Penguin (1995 edition).

Dasgupta, Amitava. *Beating Drug Tests and Defending Positive Results: A Toxicologist's Perspective*. Springer Science & Business Media (2010).

Dickinson, Simon. Insights. Cézanne and Mt Sainte-Victoire: The father of us all. https://www.simondickinson.com/2020/08/04/cezanne-mt-sainte-victoire-the-father-of-us-all/

East Carroll Parish, Lousiana Geneology. https://eastcarrollparishlouisianagenealogy.blogspot.com/2009/09/women-steamboat-captains.html

Fordham, Frieda. *An introduction to Jung's Psychology*. Penguin (1966).

Frost, Robert. 'The Road Not Taken'. *The Atlantic Monthly* (1915). First poem in the collection *Mountain Interval* (1916).

Galapagos Conservation Trust. Darwin's Finches. https://galapagosconservation.org.uk/wildlife/darwins-finches/

Government of the Netherlands, 'Set-up of first seven cannabis-growing farms for experiment has commenced'. https://www.government.nl/latest/news/2021/11/04/set-up of first seven cannabis-growing farms for experiment has commenced

Greenspan, Jesse. Why Peter the Great Tortured and Killed His Own Son. (22 August 2018). https://www.history.com/news/peter-the-great-tortured-killed-own-son

Hollis, Matthew. *Now All Roads Lead to France: the Last Years of Edward Thomas*. Faber and Faber (2011).

Holligan, Anna. Cannabis trial: Dutch cities picked for cafe supply experiment. BBC News, The Hague (30 August 2019). https://www.bbc.com/news/world-europe-49508526

Huyghe, René. Paul Cézanne, French artist. https://www.britannica.com/biography/Paul-Cezanne (updated 15 January 2022).

Household and family projections Australia 2016–2041. https://www.abs.gov.au/statistics/people/population/household-and-family-projections-australia/latest-release

Jammer, Max. *Einstein and Religion*. Princeton University Press (2002).

Jordan, Myfan. Generation Expendable, Older Women Workers in the Pandeconomy (October 2021). Grassroots Research Studio. https://www.grassrootsresearch.com.au/_files/ugd/4f0ea2_eaa29c63cfd540be99d4c9bacd2b8e50.pdf.

Kaufmann, Hans & Rita Wildegans. *Van Gogh's Ear: Paul Gauguin and the Pact of Silence*. Osburg (2008). https://vangoghsear.com/

Know One, Teach One. https://www.koto.com.au/about-koto

Lampedusa Cruises (listing created September 2018). https://www.weareonaboat.com/en/listings/631472-lampedusa-cruises-migration-tour

Letz, Margo. Singing About the Avignon Bridge. Curious Rambler (13 October 2016). https://curiousrambler.com/sur-le-pont-davignon/

Locoul, Gore Laura. *Memories of the Old Plantation Home: A Creole Family Album*. Zoe Co (2000).

Louisiana Africans, Cajun and Creole. https://gibsonsworld.com/the-africans-cajun-and-creole/

Mackellar, Dorothea (1904). 'My Country'. Poets Collective.. https://poetscollective.org/publicdomain/my-country/. The poem was first published in the London *Spectator* on 5 September 1908 titled 'Core of My Heart'. It reappeared several times in Australia before being included as 'My Country' in Mackellar's first book, *The Closed Door and Other Verses* (Melbourne, 1911). It is believed to have been directly inspired by Mackellar's love of the Allyn River district, NSW. https://www.sl.nsw.gov.au/stories/dorothea-mackellars-my-country

Malathronas, John. (28 September 2018). The Greek island where the end of the world began. CNN Travel. https://edition.cnn.com/travel/article/patmos-island-greece/index.html

Manohla, Dargis. Twin prostitutes growing old plying their trade in Amsterdam. *New York Times* (7 August 2012). https://www.nytimes.com/2012/08/08/movies/movie-review-meet-the-fokkens-a-documentary-on-dutch-sisters.html

Massie, K. Robert. *Peter the Great: His Life and World*. Weidenfeld & Nicolson (paperback, 1980).

Mitchell, Margaret. *Gone With the Wind*. Macmillan, New York (1936). The film (1939). Produced by David O. Selznick of Selznick International Pictures and directed by Victor Fleming.

Mont Sainte-Victoire Paintings (1882–1906) by Paul Cézanne. http://www.visual-arts-cork.com/paintings-analysis/montagne-sainte-victoire.htm

Murray, Ruth Beckmann, Judith Proctor Zentner, Richard Yakimo. *Health Promotion Strategies Through the Lifespan*. Pearson (8th edition, 2008).

Nadler, Stephen. 'Who tried to kill Spinoza?' *Jewish Review of Books* (Winter 2019). https://jewishreviewofbooks.com/articles/4991/who-tried-to-kill-spinoza/

Naifeh, Steven & Gregory White Smith. *Van Gogh, The Life*. Random House (paperback 2012).

National Center on Sexual Exploitation, The Netherlands. https://endsexualexploitation.org/articles/the-failure-of-legalization-of-prostitution-in-the-netherlands/

Nikel, David. 'We Are The Netherlands: Dutch Government Ditches Holland Brand'. *Forbes*. (5 October2019). https://www.forbes.com/sites/davidnikel/2019/10/05/its-netherlands-not-holland-dutch-government-decides/?sh=3fcba28d7a17

Per Capita. The Benevolent Society and the Longevity Innovation Hub. The Adequacy of the Age Pension: An Assessment of Pensioner Living Standards. (14 September 2016). https://percapita.org.au/our_work/the-adequacy-of-the-age-pension-in-australia/

Palace, Steve. 'When Audrey Hepburn Danced To Help the Dutch Resistance'. *The Vintage News* (12 May 2021) https://www.thevintagenews.com/2021/05/12/audrey-hepburns-dutch-resistance/

Schofield, Hugh. Mata Hari 'was framed'. BBC News (16 October 2001). http://news.bbc.co.uk/2/hi/europe/1602486.stm

Semmelweis, Ignaz. The father of infection control. (1818–1865), *New Scientist*. https://www.newscientist.com/people/ignaz-semmelweis/

Shawcross, Paul. Sur, or is it Sous, le Pont d'Avignon Which is it? Perfectly Provence (2020) https://perfectlyprovence.co/sur-or-is-it-sous-le-pont-davignon/

Spinoza, Baruch. *Ethica*. Written in Latin 1664–65 and published posthumously in 1677, the year of his death. George Eliot (Marian Evans, 1819–1880) prepared the earliest English translation of *Ethica* in 1854–56. The University of Nebraska – Lincoln contains electronic references to *Ethics* by Benedict de Spinoza, Translated by George Eliot, edited by Thomas Deegan (1981). Institut fur Anglistik und Amerikanistik, Universität Salzburg, Austria. https://digitalcommons.unl.edu/libelecrefmat/9/

Steiner, Rudolph. *Bees*. Steiner Books (1998).

Stone, Jon. 'Macedonia officially changes name to North Macedonia after long-running dispute with Greece'. *The Independent* (13 February 2019). https://www.independent.co.uk/news/world/europe/macedonia-north-name-change-greece-nato-controversy-eu-accession-a8776806.html

Sunshine Coast Council. Backward Glance. (31 August 2016). The history of the name Glass House Mountains. https://www.sunshinecoast.qld.gov.au/Council/News-Centre/Backward-Glance-and-the-history-of-the-name-Glass-House-Mountains-300816

The Association Het Spinozahuis. https://www.spinozahuis.nl/en/association-the-spinoza-house

The Edward Thomas Fellowship (1878–1917). https://edward-thomas-fellowship.org.uk/

Thomas, Edward. 'Adlestrop' (1917). Poetry Foundation. https://www.poetryfoundation.org/poems/53744/adlestrop

The Outdoor Museum, Home to the best Dutch Masters. https://vincentvangoghexperience.com/museum/?lang=en

The Yellow House. The Van Gogh Gallery. http://blog.vangoghgallery.com/index.php/en/2012/07/12/the-yellow-house/

The Van Gogh Walking Tour. https://www.arlestourisme.com/en/the-van-gogh-tour.html

Twain, Mark. *Life on the Mississippi*: Illustrated classic. Miravista Press (Paperback, 2018).

Tsar Peter House. https://www.iamsterdam.com/en/see-and-do/things-to-do/museums-and-galleries/museums/czar-peter-house

Wolf, Chris. 'The little-known story of Vietnamese communist leader Ho Chi Minh's admiration for the US'. *The World* (2017). https://www.pri.org/stories/2017-09-18/little-known-story-vietnamese-communist-leader-ho-chi-minh-s-admiration-us

www.ingramcontent.com/pod-product-compliance
Lightning Source LLC
Chambersburg PA
CBHW070930080526
44589CB00013B/1454